The Essential Guide to
Lesson Planning

The Essential Guide to
Lesson Planning

LEILA WALKER

PEARSON
Longman

Harlow, England • London • New York • Boston • San Francisco • Toronto
Sydney • Tokyo • Singapore • Hong Kong • Seoul • Taipei • New Delhi
Cape Town • Madrid • Mexico City • Amsterdam • Munich • Paris • Milan

Pearson Education Limited

Edinburgh Gate
Harlow CM20 2JE
United Kingdom
Tel: +44 (0)1279 623623
Fax: +44 (0)1279 431059
Website: www.pearsoned.co.uk

First edition published in Great Britain in 2008

© Pearson Education Limited 2008

The right of Leila Walker to be identified as author of this work
has been asserted by her in accordance with the Copyright, Designs
and Patents Act 1988.

ISBN: 978-1-4058-7277-5

British Library Cataloguing in Publication Data
A CIP catalogue record for this book can be obtained from the British Library

Library of Congress Cataloging in Publication Data
Walker, Leila.
    The essential guide to lesson planning / Leila Walker.
        p. cm.
    Includes bibliographical references and index.
    ISBN-13: 978-1-4058-7277-5 (pbk.)
1. Lesson planning.   2. First year teachers—In-service training.   I. Title.
    LB1027.4.W35   2008
    371.3028—dc22

2007052448

10 9 8 7 6 5 4 3 2
11 10 09 08

Typeset in 9.5/15 Interstate-Light by 73
Printed and bound in Great Britain by Henry Ling Limited, at the Dorset Press, Dorchester, DT1 1HD

The Publisher's policy is to use paper manufactured from sustainable forests.

Contents

LRC Radbrook

About the author

Dr Leila Walker is a Senior Researcher at Futurelab, a charity dedicated to transforming educational practices to meet the challenges and needs of education in the 21st century. Having researched what successful practitioners classified as excellent teaching for her PhD, followed by several years as an Advanced Skills Teacher and more recently as an Assistant Head Teacher at a secondary comprehensive, she uses her own experience to show new teachers how to plan successfully for their unique classrooms, with additional support from the educational research field.

Acknowledgements

Throughout my 15 years of teaching and researching within the education community, I have worked with some truly inspirational practitioners and researchers.

My first tentative steps into teaching and all my future career moves were inspired by my PGCE tutor at Cambridge University – Dr John Raffan.

My research years allowed me to increase my understanding of teaching and learning – allowing me to return to the classroom a more informed and skilled practitioner. Professor Kenneth Ruthven taught me the importance of research within the education field and why practitioners should continue to learn from this rich literature.

I would also like to thank all the teachers I have worked with. You are the unsung heroes of education and society and I am yet to find any profession that works harder and requires more skills than teaching.

My ultimate thanks go out to my husband Julian and my mother Joan who continue to support my varied career and, at times, obsession with work.

Introduction

The Essential Guide to Lesson Planning is intended to help trainee teachers and newly qualified teachers (NQTs) come to grips with the daily lesson planning required from them - this can be up to 20–30 lessons a week (based on 1-hour lessons). This book is founded on the premise that a good teacher will *always* plan a lesson and not simply rely on 'old' material. Each new lesson needs to be fresh and representative of the 30 young people you are responsible for and their individual needs. You may choose similar strategies and resources to those tried and tested with similar students and individuals as your years in teaching roll on - but you should always tweak and tailor approaches to match the needs of your current teaching group. *However*, you also need to survive. Planning a new lesson each time is ok but how do you do it day in, day out - term after term - without burning out? The answer is to learn the basics of good lesson planning and use this format as the foundation of all your lessons - it *will* become routine. As teachers we gradually build up our repertoire of materials and lesson plans - and we may choose to discard some in favour of others. Remember, teaching is a craft - it is learnt and shaped over time.

As a new teacher, entering a classroom of 30 young people for the first time *is* daunting. Do not be afraid of this feeling - every teacher experienced the same: if they did not I suspect they were not very good. If you are daunted it shows that you have respect for the profession you have chosen and understand the great privilege you have been given of teaching a group of young, impressionable (and often unpredictable) individuals. This feeling will also spur you on to producing great lessons. Teaching can be incredibly rewarding and it can also at times be terribly challenging - but with perseverance and (importantly) guidance you can become an excellent teacher and have a wonderfully fulfilling career.

This book will show you how the time spent planning good lessons can help to ensure that your time in the classroom and that of the 30 individuals you are in charge of is effective, productive and enjoyable. It is a simple correlation - the better prepared you are the better your lesson will be - regardless of the group. It is true that some groups you teach will be far more challenging than others - but that does not mean you spend a disproportionate amount of time planning for the more challenging groups. What you need to do is plan effectively. Planning is not simply about how you deliver a particular learning goal – it is multi-layered. How you are going to plan your space, organise your students, manage additional adult help and build in a rewards plan to reinforce good behaviour and good learning are all questions you need to address.

A key goal is to show you that planning lessons and behaviour management are not two separate entities – any good lesson plan will have built-in behaviour management strategies. If students are catered for, allowed to achieve and their good work reinforced, even the most challenging can be fun to teach.

I wish you much luck as you start out on your new career and I hope you enjoy it!

How can I use this book effectively?

The Essential Guide to Lesson Planning was written so that the reader could dip in and out of it, rather than necessarily read it straight through.

Chapter 1 will provide you with an overview of what a good lesson should entail and the different components required in planning. After that you may wish to focus on a particular part of a lesson or a specific aspect of teaching and learning, so for that reason each chapter is written as a stand alone guide to a particular planning component.

Chapters 4, 5, 6 and 7 can be read together as they cover the three main events in any lesson – starter activity, main development activity and the plenary.

Chapters 2 and 8 cover issues around the classroom environment and managing behaviour. The environment you provide for yourself and the young people you will teach within it can have a significant effect on behaviour, therefore it may be of use to read these chapters together.

Chapters 3, 9 and 10 are best read in conjunction with one another as they cover the topics of lesson planning, special educational needs, and gifted and talented. When planning lessons our key objectives must have regard to the individuals we are teaching. Therefore, we must use the information/data provided to set lesson objectives so that individuals can progress in lessons, are challenged, but are able to succeed.

Chapters 11 and 12 discuss the use of assessment for learning and homework. As these two events often overlap, with homework being marked using assessment for learning strategies, these chapters should be read together.

In every chapter you will find the following features:

- **Teaching tips** – these boxes draw out additional ideas on how to improve your planning.

- **Teaching reference** – these boxes provide you with additional teaching and learning information regarding a specific subject.

- **Research evidence** – these boxes will help you to place the guidance in a research context, useful when writing professional essays or simply wishing to know what proof there is for particular teaching and learning strategies.

- **Weblinks** – useful websites to take your learning further on a specific topic.

- **Further activity** – each chapter ends with a number of activities to help you consolidate your understanding.

Leila Walker
2008

The ABC of Lesson Planning

What will I learn in this chapter?

✔ The five parts of a successful lesson

✔ The rationale behind each part of a lesson

Throughout my 15 years of teaching I can honestly say that I was not the most creative teacher you would ever have met. However, the skill I did manage to finely tune was putting together a foolproof method for planning a successful lesson quickly. The only part of lesson planning that slows down this process is your own knowledge of the subject content to be taught but there are even short cuts with this (Chapter 5).

Ofsted guidelines

All lessons should contain the following three parts:

✔ **Starter** – here you introduce the lesson to the students through a 'warming up' activity.
✔ **Main development activity** – this is the 'main event' where most learning occurs.
✔ **Plenary** – this is where we check 'What has been learnt?'

However, in practice lessons are more complex than this. I have added two more parts that need to be thought through in your planning:

✔ **Getting students in.**
✔ **Dismissing students.**

With the introduction of a plethora of government guidelines for teaching and learning at both primary and secondary level, where essential parts of a lesson to be taught are prescribed, interpretation of these parts is still left open to the

Gagne's nine events of instruction, *The Conditions of Learning* (1965)

Gagne created a nine-step process called the events of instruction, which correlate to and address the conditions of learning.

1. Gain attention.
2. Inform learners of objectives.
3. Stimulate recall of prior learning.
4. Present the content.
5. Provide 'learning guidance'.
6. Elicit performance (practice).
7. Provide feedback.
8. Assess performance.
9. Enhance retention and transfer to the job.

There are many similarities between DCSF guidelines and Gagne's theory. It is important to understand that the basics of good teaching do not appear to change over time.

teacher. What follows is a description of the format that any good lesson should take. Later chapters will look at how each part of a lesson should be planned and give practical ideas you can use in your own classroom. However, this section simply describes the *framework* that can be used in every lesson.

The five part lesson

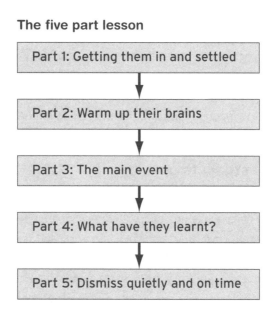

Part 1: Getting them in and settled

Many teachers omit this part of a lesson or older teachers get away with not planning it because the students already have a rapport with them. It should never be forgotten, as many trainees/NQTs are often dismayed by how students react to them compared with another teacher. It is simply that students like familiarity and teachers' names often precede them if they have a reputation of being a good or strict teacher. As a new teacher to a school this is something that you have to gain, but it can be done by being consistent with the students. Nevertheless, however responsive students are to you, a good teacher should not omit this part of the lesson.

Getting them in. It sounds obvious but in reality this can be a critical point that sets the scene for a successful or unsuccessful lesson. Students need to have boundaries and one important boundary is your classroom compared with the spaces around the school where they partake in their own activities.

Be on time for your lesson, Miss!

Students know which teachers are always in the classrooms waiting for them and those who saunter in from the staff-room with a cup of coffee in their hand. If we expect students to be on time for lessons they should expect the same from us. If you have your own classroom this is an easy task; if you are nomadic in your teaching this is much more difficult. The only way to improve time management is to ensure your last class leaves in an orderly fashion on the bell, and that any follow-up conversations with students take place before the bell or are arranged for a meeting later in the day. The latter is often better, as the student has had time to reflect on their actions and you do not have 30 other students listening in.

Line students up

Discuss with your faculty/team where the students line up for lessons. A good faculty will have this procedure already. A line up helps to encourage calm behaviour in students in preparation for your lesson and sends out a positive message about your expectations of them. It also allows you to troubleshoot any problems prior to students entering your lesson e.g. uniform, eating. If a student is still supping a hot drink from break, simply inform them that hot drinks are not allowed in the classroom and point them to the closest bin. Avoid confrontations – instead, describe what they are doing so they have to choose to take the correct action ('Joe, you have a drink in your hand.'). If a student is resisting and continues to show disruptive behaviour you can deal with them outside whilst the class enters the room – ensuring you have bell work (Chapter 4) waiting for them.

If your faculty or your teaching area appears too chaotic with other teachers not insisting on line ups you can do one of two things: first, insist your group do line up and tell them they are setting an example and this is what *you* expect because you have very high expectations, or, get them in as they arrive, ensuring you have bell work. It never ceased to amaze me how many students would turn up early for my lessons (not because they were particularly exciting) so they could get some peace and quiet from break/lunch times or some simply because they liked being praised for something quite simple (do not underestimate the power of praise – even the most disruptive of students can be made more malleable with words of encouragement). This additional five minutes with some students can produce interesting conversations about how they are getting on and helps to build your relationship with them. These 'early' students also help to set a great example to those who may think at first they can arrive late to your lesson and take their time to settle.

Deal with late arrivals

Your school should have a Teaching and Learning or Behaviour policy with action to be taken, e.g. two lates and a detention. If your school has a policy make sure you indicate to the students that you are using it and that you are noting down lates (here is where registers are invaluable – see p. 9). If your school does not have clear guidelines you need to set something in place, e.g. two lates and a phone call/letter home. Alternatively or simultaneously, use positive reinforcements such as praise phone calls/letters for 100% on time to lessons in a term. I have worked in a range of schools and in each one the phone call home appeared to have the greatest impact, particularly praise. You often forget that some of our most disruptive students get no praise in their lives, particularly from home, so this contact can be an incredibly powerful tool. It also helps you engage with parents, some of whom will be expecting a negative rather than positive message.

TEACHING TIPS

Dealing with late arrivals

✔ Don't make a scene!

✔ Acknowledge that a student is late.

✔ Usher them to their seats and point them to the current activity.

✔ Inform them that you will ask them at the end of the lesson why they were late.

Greet students as they enter the classroom

Sounds simple, and is! You don't have to be over the top and ask them questions for the sake of it, but just acknowledging them as they enter sets a welcoming atmosphere. Many students feel uncomfortable entering a classroom, especially with teachers they do not know or who they may have had a disagreement with in the past. It is important that students are given a clean slate and know that an incident that has been dealt with is in the past and they will not be labelled because of previous poor behaviour.

Cognitive fallout

Using the correct language in class is so important if you are to avoid unnecessary conflict.

Behaviour management guru Bill Rogers (2006) talks about 'primary' and 'secondary' behaviour. He claims the initial behaviour shown by students, 'primary', can be prevented from escalating to a 'secondary' level by allowing the student cognitive fallout.

Cognitive fallout is simply allowing the student thinking time to review their behaviour and to then change it without being told to – and importantly without being 'shown up' in front of the class. We have to remember we are often dealing with students who have fragile self-esteem and if we challenge them they will often resort to face-saving tactics as the image they have with their peers is more important than that with their teacher and the consequence of their behaviour.

So how do you do this? The simple rule is: *describe* their behaviour and then wait for them to change.

For example,

> *'Paul, you are chewing gum.'*
> *'Sarah, you are talking over me.'*
> *'Mike, you have not started the practical yet.'*

Don't be afraid to try this – all you are doing is giving the student a chance to change their behaviour without unnecessary escalation.

It is also important to note that greeting students is said to be an occurrence that students who are on 'action plans' automatically receive as part of their tuition on social skills. Remember that social skills are learnt on the whole by modelling the wanted behaviour.

Remove all distractions

Whether you are in the more formal setting of a laboratory or in a history classroom, students need to be encouraged to remove all distractions. There is usually a corner in a room where you can arrange for coats and bags to be placed; if you have your own classroom make this space available and obvious to help students. If you are using a classroom without such a space ask students to put everything under the table other than the equipment they need. This process should become a routine they quickly learn but will require reinforcement by praising students who automatically do it so that others can realise their mistake and quickly change their behaviour instead of being told off. In most cases pointing out those students who are modelling the correct behaviour will prevent confrontation with the others. If you see a student change their behaviour because they have noticed their mistake from what you have said, be quick to praise - not in an over the top way that will embarrass them, quick recognition will suffice.

Arrange a seating plan

Seating plans are avoided by many teachers because there is 'too much hassle and arguing involved' or 'they work better next to their friends'. Often it can feel like both arguments are valid but in fact in practice good classroom environments are often created from well thought out seating plans.

Labelling theory

'When a teacher takes a new class, he (sic) will tend to divide the class into three categories. Firstly, the "good" pupils who conform to his expectations. Secondly, the "bad" pupils who deviate. Thirdly, those who are not outstanding in either conformity or deviation. It is the names of the pupils in the first two categories that are learned immediately by the teacher. For those in the residual category, actual names are learned very much more slowly. These inferences which the teacher draws in such a highly selective way from the pupils' behaviour, and the "categorization" process to which it leads, act as a definition of the situation in which teachers and pupils find themselves. This definition provides the plan for all future interaction between the two parties.'

(David Hargreaves, *Social Relations in a Secondary School*, 1967)

This research is still relevant today over 40 years on. The assumption is that the conclusions drawn by the teacher will affect the behaviour of pupils - good and bad.

Keep this thought in mind when trying to understand student behaviour. Many students have very difficult home lives where they are not cared for appropriately and are given few boundaries. These students find conformity to school life difficult. They also often have low self-esteem, particularly about their ability - this is why you must not put students down personally - yes you can show disapproval of behaviour but not of them. This is why it is so important to explain why we have boundaries and to support those who struggle within them. This is not to say we should shift our boundaries but to provide additional intervention to help these individuals.

Simple plans can be boy/girl boy/girl or put alphabetically. Another great positive of having a seating plan is that you learn names much quicker, which is very empowering in the classroom when commenting on work or choosing participants. If you know their name you know how to contact their parents! If you have students with Learning Support Assistants (LSAs) put them together to help the LSA work with them, or alternatively, if you know you have less able students, place them with a more able one – this will benefit them both. See Chapter 8 for advice on how to work with LSAs.

A word of advice – be careful as a new teacher not to ask for too many details about your class. I have had 30 students' entire case histories that have made me terrified to even enter the classroom. What you don't know (except about their Special Educational Needs [SEN]/ability) will not hurt you because how you plan should be the same for a difficult or well-behaved class. If you have already labelled individuals before you have even taught them you are very likely to pick them out for even minor poor behaviour and then the pupil will think there is no point trying because they are expected to play up, so might as well!

Part 2: Warm up their brains

Once students are in and settled they need a warm-up act – a bit like when you go to the filming of a TV show and some poor person has to attempt to get the crowd geared up so when the 'real star' of the show appears they are jumping out of their seats with excitement. Well, unless you are a drama teacher, you may not achieve quite the same effect; however, you can get them interested in the lesson even if it is through feeling motivated by remembering what they learnt last time.

Be ready with bell work

This is a two-minute activity to enable you time to take a register and troubleshoot any issues as students enter the classroom (see Chapter 4). Alternatively, you could use a brain gym (see Chapter 4) to get them focused and their brains warmed up ready for the formal part of the lesson: these can be great fun and do not have to be subject specific. Many teachers simply ask students to write the day's date into their books and copy down the lesson's objectives.

Lesson objectives

Lesson objectives must be clearly discussed with students in the early stages of a lesson so a sense of achievement can be felt at the end. Lesson objectives are discussed in Chapter 3.

Yes, Miss! Take a register

Whilst students are engaged with bell work or even a starter activity, a register can be taken. Whether it is electronic or in paper form it is important to take a register. It can be very formal – you read out every name – this can have a very calming effect on class as you insist on silence. Alternatively, as you get to know the class or since you have a seating plan, you can call out just the names of those missing to check with the class whether anyone has seen them or not. (It never ceases to amaze me how quick students are to inform a teacher that someone is in school but skiving!)

Another positive of a register is that you can note down many important events quickly and efficiently. For example, as you take the register you can note L = lates, M = missing equipment or H = homework done. All this goes to show the class that you are in control and are organised to notice negative and positive aspects of behaviour and progress. Many schools now have praise systems so using the register here again can be useful (P = praise). A nice way to end a lesson is to read out the names of students who have worked particularly well and note this in your register. A number of praises may lead to a praise letter/phone call. Alternatively, two lates or missed equipment or missed homework may lead to a concern letter/phone call home. However, make sure what you do is in line with school policy otherwise you will have a string of complaining students and parents. If in doubt, always discuss action with your mentor/Head of Faculty or Senior Teacher in charge of the Behaviour/Teaching and Learning policy.

The starter activity

In a typical hour lesson this will take 5–10 minutes. Its purpose is to give students a flavour of the lesson and to get them thinking. Alternatively it could be an activity to elicit what they remember from a previous lesson or even a self- or peer-assessment activity where students go through their homework. (The latter is a brilliant use of time, as not only do students gain much from marking their or their peers' work, but you get a night off marking and still get to know how well your students are doing.) Greater detail about starters and their different forms is in Chapter 4.

Part 3: The main event

This stage of the lesson is where the bulk of the new learning occurs. Whatever the learning objectives are, the work needed to realise these as an outcome will happen here. Typically in an hour lesson this will take 25-40 minutes.

Powerful learning environments/De Cortes

Recent empirically supported characteristics of effective learning processes that have emerged from research on teaching and learning in general can be summarised by De Cortes' 1995 definition of a 'powerful' learning environment.

'It is a constructive, cumulative, self-regulated, goal-orientated, situated, collaborative and individually different process of knowledge and meaning building.'

The main development activity

The main development activity must aim to allow pupils to actively engage with the new knowledge/skill to be attained through Pace, Variety and Challenge (PVC). Typically this part of the lesson is where more independent learning occurs whilst the teacher monitors progress and troubleshoots individual problems. The teacher must also ensure that through variety audio, visual and kinaesthetic learners are catered for. This last point is part of the theory on 'Learning Styles' and is illustrated with the use of PVC in Chapter 5.

Part 4: What have they learnt?

With the introduction of 'assessment for learning' strategies (see Chapter 11) teachers are now well informed on how to assess student progress in class. Time is allocated to allow students to reflect on their learning, as well as checking that they have understood the key learning aim. This allows students to get a sense of achievement as well as an understanding of what they need to work on further.

The plenary

The plenary needs be no more than 10–15 minutes – but does need to happen! Even if your lesson has not gone to plan and timing has gone awry you need to attempt at least a two-minute reflection period. It will help you and the students gauge what was achieved and plan the next lesson on the back of this information. It will also allow students some sense of achievement even if the lesson appeared rushed and even manic at times.

The plenary is an activity that checks the students' learning and revisits the learning objectives. It could be as simple as a series of multiple choice questions you read out at the front or a crossword of just six or so clues. Importantly it is a cooldown stage that prepares students for the end of the lesson whilst reflecting on how their learning went. Again, peer and self-assessment are powerful tools that can be incorporated at this stage.

Part 5: Dismiss quietly and on time

However bad a lesson may be, always try to insist that there is an orderly ending so that even if control had been lost in parts the last thing the students and, importantly, you experience is having that control back – this will make you feel 110 times better when it comes to teaching the same class again. It also will be the last thing the students remember about your lesson.

Praise roll call

As mentioned earlier in the use of registers a really positive and effective ending to a lesson is to call out names of students who have done well rather than naming those who haven't (remember, it's all about modelling good behaviour). When a student comes in next lesson and says, 'Thanks for calling my mum,' the rest see that you are willing to give praise when it is due and are more likely to do well. On the other hand, when a student has received more negative feedback they may be vocal about it but the rest will see that you will follow through with acting on what you say.

Managing parental phone calls

✔ Don't be afraid to phone home. Parents tend only to be angry if teachers allow things to escalate over time without informing them of what's been happening earlier on.

✔ Log your phone call in your diary – see Chapter 7.

✔ Be polite and friendly but to the point.

✔ Tell it how it is. Describe what happened – use the words the student used. If the student used bad language, apologise to the parents that you are having to repeat it but then say what they said. The parents won't be as shocked as you think – they are more likely to be embarrassed.

✔ Try and say something positive. You think they can succeed in your lesson but they need to change their behaviour, etc . . .

✔ Ask parents to support you by discussing the incident at home.

✔ Often it is useful to report back to the parents after the next lesson – if so, write down in your diary the date you will do this. If you said you will phone – you *must* phone.

Leaving the classroom ready for the next class

Students are responsible for the space and the environment around them. Ensure that they clear up after themselves and that a pan and brush are available after cut and stick sessions. If students are resisting clearing up, stand by the door with a bin as they leave, informing them that they only leave if they make deposits into the bin. Another tip for ensuring tidiness is to control order of dismissal by the order in which the students are ready, e.g. bags packed, tidy desk, standing in silence behind their chairs.

Leave on time

Whether it is your break or you have a lesson following it is important you manage your time. Plan to have the students ready for dismissal as described about a couple of minutes before the bell – if this appears a long time you can break it up by asking questions from the lesson to test them – those who answer correctly get to leave first (particularly powerful before a break or lunch since they are usually desperate to get out). For students who you need to have follow-up chats with, arrange to do this later – say during break or in a registration time. Write down the arrangement in their journal or planner and explain the consequences for them of not appearing. Always follow up, never forget, as students quickly learn which teachers do and which don't. As you establish yourself the need for these chats will decrease.

Using lesson time to prepare for following lesson

When you have a full day of teaching ahead of you – you need to give yourself time and space in lessons to get yourself started for the next lesson. This is not to say you plan your following lesson but that you just organise yourself so you are ready for a speedy start.

✔ Get your resources out.

✔ Run through the lesson in your head.

✔ Open up relevant PowerPoint slides so you are ready to roll as the next class or session starts.

This need take no more than two minutes but helps to ensure a smooth start to the following lesson.

Summary

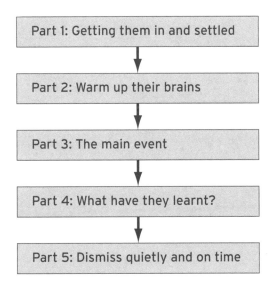

Part 1: Getting them in and settled

↓

Part 2: Warm up their brains

↓

Part 3: The main event

↓

Part 4: What have they learnt?

↓

Part 5: Dismiss quietly and on time

Further activity

Become familiar with the following websites that are specifically for teachers. Find out what each one has to offer the developing teacher:

www.standards.dfes.gov.uk

www.curriculumonline.gov.uk

www.ncaction.org.uk

www.qca.org.uk

www.teachernet.org.uk

Chapter 2

The Classroom Environment

What will I learn in this chapter?

✔ How to use displays in the classroom

✔ How to arrange your classroom to meet your and the students' needs

✔ How to manage your resources

There is no getting away from the fact that your teaching space says a lot about you as a teacher. It is important to get your teaching environment right if students are to develop the correct mindset for working as they enter your classroom and whilst they remain in it.

TEACHING TIPS

New teachers and classrooms

As teachers new to the profession or school you should be fully supported by your team and provision should be made to minimise difficulty in your first year of teaching.

One of the main hurdles is classroom allocation. I feel strongly that as a new teacher you should be given a single classroom to use where possible. More experienced teachers can cope with change better. Ask your team leader – if you don't ask they may think you don't mind!

At a minimum you should teach the same class in the same classroom so you can at least keep resources in one place.

Importantly, a good environment will help *you*. Working in a pleasant and controlled space will help you to remain calm and allow you to enjoy your own time within it – whether preparing, marking or teaching. I once spent two days of my summer holiday painting my classroom as it was in a horrible state and no amount of display would cover it. The caretakers found me a spare can of paint and in the end joined in as they couldn't stand my uselessness in painting. I don't recommend you paint but don't be shy to report a shabby environment – those who nag the most are often the first to be dealt with.

Displays

If you are fortunate enough to have your own classroom displayed material is far easier to control. However, it does require time but I think this is worth it in the long run. If you have several teaching classrooms, see if you can work with other colleagues in providing space within each one to use for your own purposes – this need be no more than a small display board.

Displays are a simple way of brightening up a room and students (even though they will often say the opposite) love seeing their work on the wall – it gives them

Raising self-esteem

Try to ensure that you show work from all the students as the year goes on . . . you don't have to display the best all the time or the neatest.

Display work from older students

The work from older students can help to raise students' expectations by providing an insight into the eventual standard required.

a sense of achievement. However, don't feel you have to be constantly updating your displays (it is time-consuming) – once a term is often enough. Ask students to help during lunchtime – there are always some who are willing. Alternatively you may have administrative staff in the reprographics team whose responsibility it is to maintain displays around the school. Hand over some work and ask them to mount it and put it on your walls – job done!

Classroom environments – interest areas

Having interest areas can increase work on particular topics. Morrow and Weinstein (1982) found that a library corner led to more involvement in literature amongst students.

My favourite display and one the students never stop coming back to look at is photos of themselves and their peers in action. You don't even have to take the photos yourself – ask someone in reprographics (they'll love you by this time) to come into a lesson and take photos. Tell the students beforehand and just check with their Head of Year to see if any have parents/carers who do not allow photos to be taken – this is important, so don't forget to ask. The great thing about photos is they can be displayed for long periods of time without appearing to date.

If you have the energy or ideally in conjunction with your department/faculty (if it is small), look at the space directly outside your classroom – usually a corridor where students line up or an outside wall. These spaces are often the scruffiest as bags are brushed against them or somehow a marker pen has made its way down

Maintaining displays

✔ Keep them simple – photos, pieces of students' work, event posters, exam dates.

✔ Use lesson time to allow students to display their work and look at peers' work.

✔ Someone in school is probably in charge of displays – hand over the work you wish to display and ask them to laminate or mount it – then to put it up in your classroom or corridor.

✔ Don't let an area get shabby – students pick up on their environment.

✔ Do use corridor space to get students interested in your subject.

the entire length of the wall! Put up displays here – but be careful to make them durable as however well behaved your students are this is a difficult area to keep smart. If students see an area kept tidy and looked after they are much more likely to show it respect and act accordingly when in that space – it also provides them with additional stimulus when lining up.

Finally, a display that the students would benefit from is that of their course details and upcoming exam dates or events . . . keep them in the know.

Seating arrangements

So you now have nice walls. But creating a powerful learning environment does not end there. Where do you place the students? Most classrooms have mobile furniture and therefore you can match the seating arrangements to suit your activity. Don't be afraid of moving furniture midway in a lesson – the two minutes they spend rearranging themselves will provide them with a short active break that will refresh them for the next stage of the lesson.

Using a double-horseshoe arrangement

This arrangement enables all students to face the front but also allows options for changing pairings or groups.

It also allows the teacher easy access around the students and closer proximity to them.

When you are requiring independent/pair work then you are best to place student desks in pairs to avoid distractions from others. For group work, get pupils to push tables together or move chairs so they are in a circle for a discussion. When you are thinking about your arrangement ensure that the end result allows you easy access around the room to troubleshoot where needed.

Keep them active!

Everybody finds it difficult to stay focused sitting in the same position for an hour, so think about your poor students. Move seats around – to your front desk for a class discussion, or to sit in groups or pairs – to help retain their attention for longer. The movement acts as a small break but also helps get their blood flowing around.

Don't forget brain gyms if students appear particularly lethargic. See Chapter 4.

Boards

Most classrooms have static boards so you would think they were always in the correct position or the correct size but this is not always the case. If you have decided to change your room around ask for your board to be taken down and rehung. Don't move everything around to suit the board if it is in the wrong place to begin with. Also, see if you can have more than one board in your room – this is really practical if you have an interactive board. The reason for having more than one is to allow you flexibility in the room but also to provide an additional space for you to keep material on whilst you change information on the other or allow students to use for their own purposes. Most importantly, make sure your boards are in a position that the students can read from. This sounds simple, but you wouldn't believe how many students have to be contortionists in order to read or copy from the board.

Creating a good display

✔ Frame your board.

✔ Back students' work so it stands out – especially if it is on white paper.

✔ Write an explanation of what the task was.

✔ Write an explanation about what is good about the work.

On your board or around it display information that you are constantly referring to, e.g. class rules or key words in the topic being taught.

If you do not have extra boards, improvise - sellotape and sugar paper can be used. When demonstrating a practical point often the best position is away from the main board. Quick solution - sellotape a large piece of sugar paper to the wall and use that to display key words as they arise or questions that need answering later.

A final useful board is one where you write the name of students who gained a consequence/sanction during the lesson. Students need to be shown clearly the outcome of their actions so whether it is a praise/reward or a consequence for poor behaviour, display it - often students complain that they did not realise they had been given the consequence.

Resources

At some point during a lesson students will require additional resources to those they are told to bring to school, although you will always have some students lacking the basics. The most effective way forward with students who have difficulty with being correctly equipped is to always have a supply to hand out. However, you are not helping them by providing them with resources each lesson. When a student forgets equipment make a note of it and in line with your school policy or, failing that, one you have agreed with your classes, make sure there is a consequence. The consequence may be a detention or a letter/phone call home for two or three occurrences of incorrect equipment. You may even suggest to their Head of Year/Pastoral Manager that a report card would be useful, as students with equipment issues will be having problems in every subject, so it needs to be centrally monitored.

Resources that you bring into the classroom need to be easily accessible - don't have glue sticks in one box and ask them to fetch one - too chaotic. Work in fours of everything. Collect ice cream tubs (good excuse to eat the stuff) and use them to hold resources such as glue and scissors. Make sure you have enough - one resource between two is usually ample. Then split the room into four and place the resources so that when students collect them they are divided by four at least. Alternatively you could have a resources monitor but getting pupils out of their seats to fetch things helps keep them awake - and is also quicker than one or two students handing things out. Importantly, count resources back in - resources are expensive so you can't afford to lose a glue stick each lesson.

Have plastic trays – you'll learn to love them. Again, have four, and provide the additional resources for the lesson on the tray and put them into your four areas for students to access them when required. At the end of the lesson you only have four trays to sort out – or ideally ask a student to do it for you.

Actions Bring Consequences

It is important that students learn that all their actions (good and not so good) will lead to a consequence. As a teacher you must try and influence this choice of action by ensuring there is a positive and negative consequence available dependent upon the behaviour shown.

So if students bring all their resources to class – at least acknowledge this to reinforce the behaviour. I have had many teachers say to me 'why should we "reward" what they are expected to do anyway?' My argument is – what is wrong with reinforcement of good choices – we are dealing with children and young adults – they look to us as adults to guide them through their decision-making.

You can read more fully about Actions Bring Consequences in Chapter 8.

Hanging space

As mentioned in Chapter 1 you need to have a defined area, if possible, for the students to hang their coats and place their bags. If the classroom you have taken over from a colleague doesn't appear to have one, create one – it needn't be the size of a cloak room. Ask the caretaker if there are some hooks they could put up or place a desk by a wall for pupils to put their belongings on. It's worth it . . . all they need on their desks are books, pens, journals, etc. They need to see your classroom as their learning space. Don't be taken in by students who claim to have valuables! Valuables shouldn't be in school or else you can keep them in a locked space in your desk. Students don't usually like handing things over so will end up placing items back into their bags.

The perfect hanging spaces are the box shelves up against the wall that fit bags and coats neatly. They are costly, but if there is some spare cash you could ask – at worst the administrators will say no.

Personal space

You need to have an area for your own resources such as teaching files. Even if you have space in an office it is useful to keep files in your classroom as occasionally you may need to pull something from them, e.g. an extension sheet if needing to provide unexpected additional work or, this sounds a bit naughty but it is realistic, during some independent activities you may find yourself with ten or so minutes where you could be usefully planning another lesson or marking some books. This may not sound professional but you have to be productive with your time. If the students are getting on and do not appear to need your additional guidance, do something to fill the time rather than sitting at your desk or wandering about just staring at them.

Organise your class books. Using large plastic containers or cardboard boxes with the name of the class is simple, useful and creates a sense of organisation quickly. It is an easy way for students to hand in books or keep them in class and then get them at the start of a lesson with little fuss. It also prevents books from getting lost - something that very easily happens. Containers and boxes allow you to easily carry your books home with you if that is where you decide to do your marking.

Class books – who keeps them?

If you have space, always take books in after a lesson (unless they are needed for homework) as this will cut down on the chance of students forgetting their book next time.

Certain groups are prone to organisational problems and it may be best to keep a class book in class at all times and a separate home book or homework book. There is nothing worse than having to hand out sheets of paper each lesson that will eventually go missing.

However, having said that, students must learn to take responsibility – so if you have a good class or you fancy a challenge, let them have their books. If you do this you must be prepared to take action with students who forget their books, with appropriate sanctions. Call their parents and ask them to help the kids pack their bags. If you have a particular student concern and you are not their tutor or Head of Year/Key Stage Manager, ask the teacher in charge of pastoral studies to check that this is not a whole school issue with this student that needs a more holistic approach.

If you are a nomadic teacher, having boxes to hold books is useful as you go from one classroom to another. Unless your school is particularly mean you should at least teach the same class in the same classroom so the box can stay in that room if need be. Another good thing about these boxes is that you invariably have spare sheets or copies of work you have used in that lesson but as you move from one lesson or class to another (unless you are unbelievably organised) you can deposit copies into the box and file them at the end of term.

Plants! Give students some additional oxygen . . .

Plants are a cheap way of cheering up your room – making it welcoming and in addition providing you and your students with some extra oxygen. A word of advice though – the plants need to be hardy, as unless you are a very caring gardener in your leisure time you'll forget about them and they will add to the drabness of your room as they wilt and die. My favourite – mother-in-law's tongue!

Summary

✔ Use displays to brighten up your learning environment – classroom and outside corridor.

✔ Use photos, students' work (current and old), posters and information on their curriculum including important dates, e.g. exam dates.

✔ Use additional boards in the classroom to provide you with flexibility.

✔ Arrange your seating to suit the class activity – don't be afraid to move it during a lesson.

✔ Tray up resources × four to spread out access for students.

✔ Label up boxes/trays per class or subject. Use these boxes to keep class books in or additional resources that will need filing when you have time.

✔ Keep your own teaching resources in the classroom to provide yourself with easy access during a lesson.

✔ Allocate an area in your classroom where the students can hang their bags and coats.

Further activity

Start collecting resources to use for displays. Material could come from newspapers, magazines, internet, free posters, etc . . .

Keep in mind topics you will be covering within a key stage or subject. It is really useful to collect everyday information that relates to what you will be teaching in the classroom.

Chapter 3

Lesson Objectives

What will I learn in this chapter?

✔ How to write a good lesson objective

✔ How to incorporate lesson objectives into your lesson

✔ How to use key words

✔ What a SMART target is

Teachers have always used lesson objectives when planning a lesson since these are, at their simplest level, what you have decided the students are going to learn about. However, it was not always the case that these objectives were shared with the class. The primary rationale for having objectives is that they provide the teacher with an invaluable assessment tool to measure the success of the lesson and give guidance for follow-up work. The use of lesson objectives in 'assessment for learning' is discussed in detail in Chapter 11. A second rationale that carries much weight is the motivational benefit objectives bring with them – the student leaving the class having a sense of achievement if they have partially or fully met the objectives acts as a powerful reinforcement for the following lesson.

Vygotsky, zone of proximal development

Lev Vygotsky's notion of the 'zone of proximal development' is the gap between a learner's current or actual development level and the learner's emerging or potential level of development.

'The distance between the actual development level as determined by independent problem solving and the level of potential development as determined through problem solving under adult guidance, or in collaboration with more capable peers.'

(Vygotsky, 1978, p 86)

As teachers we must understand the students' prior knowledge and allow them to develop their thinking to a higher level but one that they are capable of reaching.

Sharing objectives and lesson outcomes is not only good practice but an explicit part of teaching in the Ofsted (Office for Standards in Education) framework. However, how lesson objectives are shared with the class and the language teachers use vary widely. Much of this variety appears to stem from the subject being taught, the age of the students and their ability. What really matters is using objectives that make sense to you and your students – if they can't understand the objective they will not know what is expected of them now or in future lessons. Understanding how you have learnt something is an important part of intellectual growth – this process is called metacognition (see Chapter 7).

Learning should be GOAL-ORIENTATED

'Meaningful learning is facilitated by an explicit awareness of the orientation towards a goal.'

(De Cortes, 1995)

Learning objectives should state what the student is expected to learn rather than be a description of the activity they are to undertake. There are two types of learning objectives:

- Objectives that focus on *what the pupil will learn*. For example, Describe the process of photosynthesis.

- Objectives that focus on *how the learning will take place*. For example, Use information from a website to find out facts about photosynthesis.

Matching learning objectives to schemes of work

When teaching you should be working from a scheme of work your team/ faculty have written. If you are unfortunate, you may join a team with no schemes of work (this is rare unless you are starting up a new curriculum; if this is the case it is best to put one together before planning individual lessons).

The QCA (Qualifications and Curriculum Authority) website is a great place to start looking for scheme of work ideas – they include individual lesson plans with lesson objectives.

http://www.standards.dfes.gov.uk/schemes3/

If you have a scheme of work you need to develop lesson objectives from this.

✔ What are the key concepts, skills to be learnt?

✔ Convert key ideas into objective statements.

Importantly, never go over the top with objectives. Some teachers give out five or more learning objectives in a lesson – this is simply too much and complicates the learning. If you have this many objectives you need to ask yourself, 'Am I trying to cover too much in the lesson?' If you have a double lesson – say two hours – you may cover this number of objectives, but do not give them to the students in one go. Divide the double into two single lessons – otherwise you and the students will lose track and be waiting a long time to assess progress. Two or three objectives should be aimed for in the majority of lessons.

Learning objectives can be used to show differentiation amongst the students' learning. A classic example is to use one of the following:

> You **MUST** have
>
> You **SHOULD** have
>
> You **COULD** have

> **ALL** students will have
>
> **MOST** students will have
>
> **SOME** students will have

In the above examples teachers gradually grade the difficulty in learning to be achieved. In practice this can take time to master but when teaching mixed ability classes is very useful, particularly when thinking through the learning needs of individuals, i.e. ensuring everyone is catered for and importantly can feel some sense of achievement. In addition, you can use level and grade indicators next to lesson objectives to signpost to students where their learning is with regards to exam attainment – many students are very motivated by this process. It is also an

An example of lesson objectives from a KS2 history lesson

> To **name** people from the past who were famous and **explain** what they were famous for.
>
> To **describe** the clothes worn a long time ago.
>
> To **describe** what is different about the clothes worn by Florence Nightingale compared with women of all generations today.

invaluable way of reminding students what level or grade they are working at – invaluable because the more informed students are about their progress the better choices it is hoped they will make in class.

As previously stated, choosing the correct language is imperative when expressing objectives. Teachers have devised a plethora of ways for phrasing objectives. A very common method for expressing objectives and outcomes has been the introduction of WALT and WILF (often shown as two characters).

WALT – What Are We Learning Today . . .
WILF – What I'm Looking For is . . .

With limited space in many classrooms teachers often have WALT and WILF laminated onto cards that are stuck next to or on their main boards so they can write their objectives easily each lesson. If you are a nomadic teacher these are convenient cards to carry round with you (with some Blu Tak!).

TEACHING TIPS

All lessons should have objectives whatever the class

Whoever you are teaching and whatever activity they are undertaking you need to give out at least one objective so students can measure their success at the end.

It is not uncommon for teachers to miss out objectives for sixth formers or just brush over them. What is good practice for one student is good practice for them all.

If you have an activity that appears to expand over more than one lesson, students need to be reminded of the objectives. However, even long-term projects need objectives to show progression as the lessons go on – they should not always be faced with exactly same ones.

More recently there has been conflict within pedagogical circles as to how best we should express learning objectives. The main argument is between those who think it is best to differentiate objectives (ALL, MOST, SOME) and those who believe this method shows a lack of sensitivity to lower achievers and may be detrimental to their motivation. The latter theorists prefer the use of general objectives that allow a teacher to differentiate discreetly through assessment of work during the lesson. My view is that *both* work in class – I have used differentiated objectives more often because I find that students see the differentiation as a ladder and if they go up the rungs they gain a higher sense of achievement, whereas other students are often just as motivated to reach one objective as any achievement is a great enough reward to keep them interested.

Useful sentence structures for general lesson objectives

To know how/about ....

To describe .... using ....

To explain .... using ....

To show how ....

To illustrate how ....

To understand how/why ....

To name ....

To define ....

Defining common words used in lesson objectives

It is worth having a poster on display in your classroom of the meaning of key words used in lesson objectives. For example, describe or explain . . . This will benefit students when they are sitting test papers/exams, allowing them to distinguish between instructional terms.

How to use lesson objectives in the classroom

So you have written your objectives on the board for all the students to see. Job done? No! A common mistake made by teachers is to just list the objectives on the board – maybe even pointing to them, asking the students to read them or even to write them down in their class books (the latter is fine if you are using it as a calming process at the start of a lesson – see bell work, Chapter 4). However, this is simply not good enough – here teachers are making the great assumption that the students have fully understood what it is that is expected of them.

Review your teaching and learning policy

All schools should have a teaching and learning policy – often found in the staff handbook. The policy should give you guidelines on the best use of objectives. Your school may be prescriptive and insist on a particular style. Make sure you check!

At the start of your lesson – probably after you have completed the bell work – you need to spend *time* on describing the objectives to the class. You can use this opportunity to move the class around the front of your desk (getting them active!) and then ask individuals to read through an objective. Next, clarify what was meant by the objective and describe the activity the students will be carrying out in order to achieve it. This can become a routine in all your lessons and provide you with a much wanted calm start.

Another useful activity you can use is to ensure that your first objective is covered by the starter activity – this means that ten minutes into the lesson you can inform the students that they have already achieved an objective in the hope it may provide the motivational impetus for the remainder of the lesson.

Finally, lesson objectives should be revisited in the plenary part of your lesson. This enables you and the students to assess what has been achieved. A neat way of getting a rough guide to achievement is to give pupils traffic light cards (red, amber and green) – here you ask students to show the card that best matches what they know about the objective (red – nothing, amber – something, green – fully understand). Of course they won't necessarily be truthful but you may also be surprised by their openness in front of peers if you have provided an environment where they feel secure in saying, 'I don't understand yet . . .' Chapter 7 discusses in detail the use of lesson objectives in plenaries.

Personal workbooks

Give low attainers' personal workbooks to record new words. Often students with low reading ages have additional literacy lessons. These books can be useful for LSAs to go through key words with them during these lessons.

Key words

When discussing lesson objectives it is useful to give out the key words that will be used in the lesson at the same time. Key words are essential for improvements in literacy whichever subject or age group you are teaching. You can either list the key words at the bottom of your learning objectives, highlight them if they appear in your learning objectives, or put them on flashcards and stick them around your board.

Raising the profile of key words in a lesson

A strategy you can use in class is to ask students to raise their hand every time a key word is used. This is a simple way of raising the profile of these words and encouraging their use.

Key words are used to complement the students' learning by providing them with the technical vocabulary of the subject.

Setting SMART targets

SMART targets are most often associated with mid- to long-term objectives. It is very good practice to ask students to set themselves (with your guidance) topic or term targets. These targets can be written in their class books at the start of a piece of work/project and revisited at the end.

> **Specific** – they say exactly what they mean.
>
> **Measurable** – you can prove that you've reached them.
>
> **Achievable** – you can reach them in the next few weeks.
>
> **Realistic** – they are about action you can take.
>
> **Time-related** – they have deadlines.

Summary

✔ Share lesson objectives with class at the start of the lesson.

✔ Explain lesson objectives and link to lesson activities.

✔ Lesson objectives should focus on **what** the students will learn or **how** the learning will take place.

✔ Common objectives used – WALT and WILF:
   What are we learning today . . .
   What I'm looking for is . . .

✔ Common objectives used to differentiate learning:
   You MUST . . . You SHOULD . . . You COULD . . .
   ALL . . . MOST . . . SOME . . .

✔ Provide students with key words to help them use the correct language during the lesson.

✔ Use SMART targets when setting students mid- to long-term goals.

Further activity

Create a poster showing students what key words used in lesson objectives mean. Make sure your definitions match the reading age of your target audience.

Key words to define may be:

   To understand . . .

   To name . . .

   To define . . .

   To illustrate . . .

   To show . . .

   To explain . . .

   To describe . . .

Chapter 4

Bell Work and Starter Activities

What will I learn in this chapter?

✔ How to incorporate 'bell work' into your lesson planning

✔ How to use 'brain gyms' to keep students' learning active

✔ Examples of bell work, brain gyms and starter activities

Fifteen years ago the terminology of 'bell work' and 'starter activity' did not appear in many PGCE (Postgraduate Certificate in Education) course's vocabulary. However, the importance of starting the lesson with something specific to 'catch their attention' was. The fundamental need to ensure, as a teacher, that you understand students' prior knowledge has always been part of a successful lesson. Commonly, teachers tested students' prior knowledge through the use of a question and answer session on knowledge/skills that were taught in the previous lesson. All that has really changed is that with DCSF/Ofsted guidance on good lesson planning there are now specific labels for the different parts of a lesson.

Bloom's taxonomy

Starter activities are mental 'warm-ups' – they need to actively engage students and provide them with high-level thinking opportunities. Bloom's taxonomy provides a useful model for creating successful starters. The six levels in his model fall into two divisions:

1. Activities and questions that involve remembering, checking on understanding and the application of knowledge – knowledge, comprehension and application.
2. Activities and questions that involve high order critical and creative thinking – analysis, synthesis and evaluation.

Bell work

Bell work, as the name implies, is an activity set at the very start of the lesson, in fact at the point where many teachers are waiting for the latecomers to enter or the last remaining students to settle and have their names read out during the register. Bell work leaves no time wasted in a lesson as it is in operation as soon as the student enters the classroom. After a short period of time students expect this event and the calm start to your lesson becomes routine. The beauty about bell work is that it allows the students who are already motivated to get on with their studies straight away; it encourages others to speed up the process of removing coats and bags etc, and actually settling down as they follow the example of the first group. Finally, bell work gives you time to deal with more challenging behaviour if it arises whilst allowing the other students to get on with their work.

Bell work is often confused with the starter activity and in fact the two can cross over if the latter requires no or little explanation and can be started as students enter the classroom. As a discrete entity the bell work should be no longer than five minutes – longer at the beginning of the year as your classes get used to this activity and used to you. The behaviour management you have to deal with at the start of the teaching year should decrease as your classes settle and their expectations of their own behaviour rise.

Bell work should be simple as it requires no input from you other than a note on the board instructing students what to do, or a piece of paper on their desk or handed to them as they enter the classroom. The latter is best used if you are rushing from one room to another and the class are already waiting outside for you – it saves you writing on the board and shows the class that you are ready from the start. It also clearly indicates that they are entering a learning zone and this is the work they must do – it gives them a sense of immediacy.

TEACHING TIPS

First lesson – explain to students what they should expect in your class

Use time in your first lesson to explain to students how your classes work. For example, if you plan to use bell work, explain that as they enter the class there will always be work ready for them to start etc . . . If you want to explain why, say you want them to be learning every second they are in your classroom!

So what are examples of bell work? The easiest and least imaginative is the copying down of the date, title of the lesson and lesson objectives. This is a good fallback if you have not been able to plan an alternative as it is still a useful process to enable the students to settle down ready to learn. If you are a language teacher this is a very useful exercise as the students can write their own date in the chosen language and even add today's weather conditions – so you see there are variations on simple ideas with a little thought.

Other bell work examples are:

- Gap-filling exercise eliciting prior knowledge from a previous lesson.
- Word search to identify key words for the lesson – helps with spelling.

- Show photos/pictures - ask students to write down words that the pictures evoke.
- A sketch in Art/Tech to elicit creativity.
- A warm up in PE.
- A discussion between pairs to elicit what they were learning last lesson or to write down key words from last lesson.
- A topic title/word or a picture on board/desks - pairs write down what they know about the topic already.
- Homework discussion - pairs swap homework and read the other's work and make verbal/written comments as instructed.
- Brain gyms - see below.

Brain gyms

A brain gym is an exercise to 'clear the cobwebs' and get the students thinking - sometimes laterally. There are many examples and the great thing about them is that they do not need to be subject specific and can occur at different points in a lesson. If you feel the lesson has lost its pace and things need picking up with a short burst of something different, use a brain gym - particularly useful in breaking up a double lesson.

An example of a brain gym

It's more powerful than God.
It's more evil than the Devil.
The poor have it.
The rich need it.
If you eat it you will die.
What is it?

Answer: Nothing

Brain gyms
www.braingym.org.uk

Some brain gyms are specifically designed to activate both halves of the brain: here are two lovely examples:

This exercise helps improve blood flow to 'switch on' the entire brain before a lesson begins. The increased blood flow helps improve concentration skills required for reading, writing, etc.

Stretch one hand so that there is as wide a space as possible between the thumb and index finger.

Place your index and thumb into the slight indentations below the collar bone on each side of the sternum. Press lightly in a pulsing manner.

At the same time put the other hand over the navel. Gently press on these points for about two minutes.

This exercise helps coordinate right and left brain by exercising the information flow between the two hemispheres. It is useful for spelling, writing, listening, reading and comprehension.

Stand or sit. Put the right hand across the body to the left knee as you raise it, and then do the same thing for the left hand on the right knee just as if you were marching.

Just do this either sitting or standing for about two minutes.

If you have challenging classes try bell work – all students need clear, bounded routines but difficult students require this even more since it is often the lack of boundaries in their lives that has led to their disruptive attitude. Challenging students are more likely to modify their behaviour if they have peers modelling what they should be doing. Of course the use of praise for doing even the simplest things, like 'Well done class for coming in so quietly and getting on with your work,' is better than telling off a couple of individuals for not doing so. Obviously those not doing as you wish need to be confronted, but using the language of choice ('You have chosen to . . . You can choose to . . . '). The key is to provide the students who are doing the correct thing with your attention and as soon as somebody else changes their behaviour/action for the better gently acknowledge it and move on so as not to go over the top. This last point is discussed in more depth in Chapter 7.

Starter activities

Concept loops/chase cards

The idea behind this activity is that students show their understanding by making links between key words. This is great for checking prior knowledge as it will show gaps in understanding or simply reinforce what they already know.

KS2 History concept loop cards

✔ Discuss the words/names below with your partner.

✔ Put them in an order to tell a story.

✔ Go through the story and be prepared to tell it to the rest of the class.

Roman Empire	Rome	Emperor
Julius Caesar	Claudius	
Roads	Sewers	Britain
Celts	Invasion	Boudicca

True or false

Simply give the students five to ten statements and ask if they are true or false. This is a quick method to use when wishing to assess students' prior knowledge. To extend the exercise ask students to explain why the statement is false – this further tests their understanding and checks that they have a rationale behind their response.

True or false quiz – gravity

If your answer is false, explain.

	True	False
1. Mass is measured in Newtons.	❏	❏
2. Gravity is a force that acts between two objects.	❏	❏
3. Weight is the amount of stuff you are made up of.	❏	❏
4. You weigh more on the moon than on the Earth.	❏	❏
5. You will sink in the sea if your weight is greater than the upthrust of the sea water.	❏	❏
6. Salty water can float heavier objects than fresh water.	❏	❏
7. Air can cause upthrust.	❏	❏
8. The further away two objects are the stronger the gravitational force between them.	❏	❏
9. The larger an object the greater the force of gravity.	❏	❏

Crosswords

Probably one of my all-time favourites – students love them (as long as they are not impossible) and they are easy to put together. Crosswords are a great literacy tool – whether you want to check their understanding/meaning of key words or to use them for spelling exercise. The website to use is **www.discoveryschool.com**. If you wish to go straight to puzzlemaking try **http://puzzlemaker.school. discovery.com**. Please try it! It really is easy – you can write a crossword in minutes or choose a different puzzle – see below.

- Maths square.
- Criss cross (crossword).
- Mazes.
- Hidden messages.
- Word searches.
- Cryptograms.
- Letter tiles.
- Fallen phrases.

Microbes and Disease

Across

4. Released by white blood cells to fight disease.
6. Atheletes foot is caused by this microbe.
8. Our body's defence for fighting disease.
9. A common complaint caused by a virus.
10. Type of blood cells that help our body fight disease.
11. Taken to boost your immunity against viral disease.
12. A microbe that reproduces by dividing up.

Down

1. Dish used to investigate microbe growth.
2. Worn by first aiders to protect themselves from disease.
3. This microbe is the smallest on all - they all cause disease.
4. Medicine taken to destroy bacteria.
5. A bacteria that causes food poisoning.
7. An organism that needs a microscope to be seen.

Don't forget that these activities are great for end of term when you wish to be seen doing a 'learning activity' rather than showing yet another video. Just make it competitive - with a small prize at the end.

Traffic light challenge

The traffic light challenge allows you in an instant to assess what all your students know already. All you do is cut out small squares of green, orange/amber and red card - then tie together with a tag. Give a pack of cards to each student - or to pairs if you wish them to discuss answers between themselves first. Ask a question - all students who know the answer show a green card, if they don't know it they hold up a red card and if they are not sure about their answer they show an amber card. As the teacher you need to randomly choose students whichever colour they hold. For example, check a green card holder did know the answer, maybe the amber card holder just needs more confidence, and do not forget the red card holder – they may just need a little help to elicit the answer.

Keeping traffic cards

The great thing about the traffic light cards is that they are easy to use. There will be times in your lessons when you need to change an activity, check what has been learnt so far or fill in some time. Keep a set of these cards in your teaching desk or resources box (if nomadic) so that you can bring them out anytime.

Mini whiteboards

Mini whiteboards allow you to check what students know either by asking them questions or by getting them to draw a picture of what they think something is like, etc. Students love writing on these rather than in their books – probably because they are not permanent.

Cheap mini whiteboards

A cheap way of producing whiteboards is to laminate a piece of A4 paper!

They can also be used for students to write their own questions, then they pass their board to a peer who attempts to answer them. This is a great way of getting students working together, testing what each other knows – plus you don't need to do any preparation.

Splat

Place words/names/numbers on your board or screen. Then ask two students to stand at the board. The aim of the game is for the student to point or 'splat' the word on the board first when a question has been asked. You can play this as a whole class by dividing the class into two and having two different players for each question come up to the board. Again you combine fun with learning and you get the students out of their seats.

Religious studies KS3

Islam	Koran	Prophet	Mohammed	Allah	Peace
Angel Gabriel		Mecca	Ramadan	Moses	Muslims
Pillars	5	Pilgrimage	Rebecca	Abraham	Jesus

Blockbusters

'I'll have a "p" please, Bob!' If you can't remember the kids' quiz 'Blockbusters', ask your parents – it was a classic! Great as a whole class activity – you put a grid together (this can be done on the board or from a projector) and within the grid are acronyms for an answer, e.g. in the grid maybe a single letter P and the question is, 'What P is a South American country?' Alternatively, you could put in the grid HP, with the question, 'What is the name of JK Rowlings' wizard schoolboy hero?' The aim of the game is to complete a line – similar to Bingo. You can split the class into two and have them compete against each other – one group has to make a horizontal line, the other a vertical.

The grid can be as large or small as you like. If you have equal teams or are playing as a whole class ensure the grid is a square. The original TV game used to have one player against two playing on a grid that was four by five. The single player has to get four across the board whilst the double player has to get five across. This latter grid is useful if you wish to put gifted and talented students against the rest of the class – it can be fun!

Example of a Blockbuster grid

PP	JL	BKL	QE
ER	AB	F	L
Z	K	SS	KA
WR	JGD	D	HS

AB – Who was Henry VIII's second wife?
QE – The name of Anne Boleyn's daughter?
F – Anne Boleyn's nationality?
and so on.

Mix and match

This exercise can be used to provide the key words for the lesson or to elicit key words from a previous lesson. Simply mix up key words and their definitions and ask the students to match them up. A mathematical alternative would be to have sums and final answers mixed up or a historical alternative would be to mix up characters with dates or historical relevance, etc.

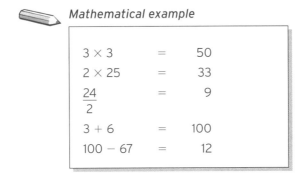

Mathematical example

3×3	=	50
2×25	=	33
$\dfrac{24}{2}$	=	9
$3 + 6$	=	100
$100 - 67$	=	12

Guess the key word/number/character

We used to call this 'Bottelini' as kids. On a Post-it write a key word, a number, a date or a character (historical or fictional), then place onto a student's head so they cannot see what it reads. Then in pairs, small groups or as a whole class, students have to guess what is written on their head by asking questions of their peers which can only have a 'yes' or 'no' response. Again, this activity injects some fun into a lesson whilst being a valid learning experience for the students.

Washing lines

Washing lines allow you to display sequences. These sequences may be numbers, dates, character appearances, chronological order of events, etc - good for science and the humanities.

Jumbled words/sentences

A great one for literacy. Write five key statements about a topic and then jumble up the words in each sentence so that they make no sense. Students are then asked to rearrange the words so they have proper sentences. Again, great for checking prior understanding. Alternatively, choose key words for the lesson but mix up the letters. The students then have to rearrange the letters to reveal the key word.

KS2 Citizenship – Media

zaneigma	(magazine)
vsiionleet	(television)
nwesppaer	(newspaper)
eetnrnit	(internet)

Word bag

I have used this with all key stages and abilities – you cannot get away from key words – you just need to differentiate and adjust the difficulty to meet the needs of the group. Basically, put some key words/characters on paper/card and place them in a bag. Students then pass the bag around and pick out a word, etc. The aim is for students to describe what they understand by the word or what they know about the character.

Show me

Some topics have 'props' that can help elicit from the students what they know on the subject. Place the 'props' in a bag and pass it around the students. Students pull out a 'prop' and explain what they know about it.

Timings and starters

It is very easy to run over with time during starter activities because they are going so well or a discussion is going on for longer than you imagined.

But for every extra minute you take on the starter you are taking one away from the plenary. The plenary *always* appears to suffer! However, the plenary is a crucial part of the lesson and must not be limited due to poor timing.

This is not an exhaustive list and you will find great ideas from other teachers in your school so make sure there are times set in meetings to share ideas and resources – if new to the school suggest this is part of a five to ten minute slot in one of your regular meetings, e.g. NQT or Mentor meetings.

It is also worth pointing out that many of the activities suggested here are transferable to the plenary part of a lesson – see Chapter 7.

Summary

✔ Bell work is a short activity that encourages students to settle quickly.

✔ Use brain gyms to keep lessons fresh by getting the students active.

✔ A good starter activity should give the students a taste of what the lesson is about.

✔ Keep starters short and sweet – don't allow them to overrun at the expense of your plenary.

Further activity

You are about to start teaching about Henry VII and wish to find out what your group already know about him. Plan a starter activity lasting five to ten minutes to elicit students' prior knowledge.

Chapter 5

Main Development Stage - Part 1

What will I learn in this chapter?

✔ How to translate curriculum content into learning activities

✔ How to inject pace, variety and challenge into your lessons

✔ How to incorporate different 'learning styles' into your planning

✔ How to use lesson templates

It is during the main development stage that the majority of new learning occurs. Therefore, even if you have perfected the art of settling down students ready to learn and invigorated them with a thought-provoking starter, this part is what really determines whether their learning is advanced or not. As mentioned in Chapter 1 this part is what takes the longest to plan – not simply because it is the longest section of the lesson but because it involves the teacher translating the bulk of the needed subject knowledge into activities from which the students will gain most learning opportunities.

Learning needs to be CONSTRUCTIVE

This implies that the acquisition of new knowledge and skill is an active process in the sense that it requires cognitive processing by the learner.

(De Cortes, 1995)

There are several characteristics of a successful main development activity. It must have PVC – be Pacey, be Varied and offer Challenge to the learner. It must also provide audio, visual and kinaesthetic opportunities where possible in order to suit the varied learning styles the students individually prefer.

Learning needs to be SITUATED

This stresses that learning occurs in interaction with social and cultural contexts and especially through participation in cultural activities and practices.

'Social interactions (particularly those that take place between the children themselves) may facilitate the course of development by exposing a child to other points of view and to conflicting ideas which may encourage him to think or re-view his ideas.'

(Cobb et al, 1991)

Subject knowledge to student activity

As a new teacher this can be the most daunting part of planning – most people outside teaching would think that as a teacher in a certain subject or for a specific year group you already have the necessary knowledge – but for some this can be what causes us the most concern as we attempt to learn new knowledge for ourselves and then translate it into an activity where others can learn from us. Be reassured that as the curriculum evolves all teachers, however bright or experienced, have to 'read up' on new knowledge or skills at some point. So how can this process be made easier and less time-consuming?

Be clear you know what the students need to know by reading the relevant National Curriculum section or exam board specification – sounds obvious, but many new teachers will rely on a Scheme of Work that the school or department has produced. It is important that you know exactly what is needed so that you don't teach pupils any less or more than they need. This last part may appear controversial but when you are teaching something you are not an expert in it's best to teach the essentials rather than risk confusion with unnecessary add-ons – also, there is an issue of time. Any teacher will tell you that being a teacher is similar to being a racehorse – getting through the curriculum or specification in time for exams or simply by the end of the year deadline is an achievement in itself.

A very good use of time is producing overall plans for the year for your classes that can simply include date (week beginning), topic being covered, knowledge/skills content, homework (optional) and exam dates. These are invaluable – as they really keep your teaching on track and quickly inform you when time is slipping. If you have a copy of the National Curriculum or specification in front of you, all you need do is divide it into the number of weeks you will be teaching for the year against the dates.

TEACHING TIPS

Scheme of work

A scheme of work (SOW) usually takes the form of a bespoke series of lesson plans that have been produced by a school/faculty/team to cover a section of the National Curriculum or an exam board specification.

The QCA has produced a series of SOW that covers the National Curriculum criteria. You can access this online at: **www.standards.dfes.gov.uk**

To provide some flexibility always plan per week rather than per lesson – working on the assumption that you have x number of lessons per week with that class or on that subject. Yes, at times a lesson will not run as planned and an additional one may have to be put in, but there will also be occasions when you have allocated too much time to a subject and time is caught up. Please write these plans – they will give you much confidence as you will have an overview of the year. See p. 60 for an example.

See p. 60 for an example.

The National Curriulum

'The National Curriculum (NC) defines the minimum educational entitlement for pupils of compulsory school age (5–16 years). It is a statutory requirement that requires all state schools to provide pupils with a curriculum.'

(www.teachernet.gov.uk)

Your school/PGCE course tutor should give you a copy of the NC that covers the key stage/subject you plan to teach. You can also find it online, **www.nc.uk.net**

As for specific lessons, once you are clear on the knowledge to be taught the first places to look for help are in course textbooks, schemes of work, websites (QCA and exam boards) and exam papers. These resources will provide you with an understanding of the level of knowledge required – all you need is the same level of understanding, don't feel you have to know more. If a student asks you something which is related but outside the knowledge required you can save face in two ways: tell them that you will find out for them ready for next lesson or ask them to find out the answer and present it to the class then. Always say 'thank you' and 'what a great question' to these students because we must encourage them all to think outside the box. You will, over time, naturally learn more than you need about a topic but to begin with it is survival that is required.

Once you are happy you have understood what it is the students must also understand, you must then choose an activity within which this learning can occur. Look through the resources your school has already – there is no point reinventing a worksheet, etc if there is an excellent one already available. Eventually you may wish to revamp one but in the meantime take advantage of the huge number of resources available. There are a number of resource books for teachers and these are often worth purchasing – **www.amazon.com** is worth a search. If you have no money to spend on resources but find some useful ones, ask your line manager if there is anything in the budget to cover such items. Much of the ICT software made for schools can be paid for on e-learning credits (a sum given to each school annually to pay for such items) – so if you find something that is good ask your school to buy it (often this budget is looked after by the school's IT manager). The internet is a great source of information if you search correctly. The QCA/exam board websites are good starting points as they will have suggested activities and resource links. In addition, if you put into a Google search the key stage you are teaching, followed by the topic, you may come across some excellent resources published by teachers: save them in your favourites folder for next time.

Using the NC to write a lesson

The NC is compartmentalised into key stages and then subjects/key skills.

It is usually presented as a series of statements that need to be addressed in your teaching.

E.g. English KS1

Speaking

1. To speak clearly, fluently and confidently to different people, pupils should be taught to:
   speak with clear diction and appropriate intonation

As the teacher you need to interpret this statement as an activity where this skill may be taught and learnt.

A final tip: remember you only need to be one lesson ahead of the students as long as you have a long-term plan, as discussed earlier. Read over the whole topic by skim reading to get a feel for it, then read specific parts in detail, bit by bit, as you plan each lesson. Remember, your knowledge, like the students', gets better

Using colleagues' knowledge

Don't be shy to ask a colleague for advice, ideas or even resources. Most teachers are flattered to be asked and will happily help out.

Ask to observe a colleague: Tell them which lesson you would like to observe and explain why. Maybe you need to see how a particular topic is taught or how to engage a difficult group or even to challenge gifted and talented students.

When you do observe, make sure you say 'thank you' and say what you thought was positive. We can all find faults in others' lessons but giving feedback is a skill, so unless you are confident you will not offend don't start giving advice if it is not wanted! Remember, you were a guest in that lesson.

with time and the following year when you come to teach the topic again you will need less time to prepare and you will be able, if you want, to read around the topic more.

PVC – pace, variety and challenge

Pace

Throughout your lesson you need to ensure there is pace. Due to the length of the main development stage it is particularly important that activities here are punchy and are not allowed to drag on unnecessarily. The main rationale behind using pace in lessons is two-fold: first it ensures learning is efficient with little or no time wasted and second, it helps maintain behaviour as it provides little or no time for distractions. Students must be occupied and on task at all times otherwise you are asking a lot from even the most studious. So how can you add pace? Break up the activity into short snappy segments – instead of one whole activity that takes up 40 minutes. Provide students with time checks – keep reminding them what it is they are expected to have achieved and how long they have left to do this. Finally, there is nothing to stop you pausing the activity at times to see how everyone is progressing and asking questions about what they have learnt so far or asking them to read out any work they have done so far – it will help give students confidence that they are on the right track or give others a needed reminder of what they need to do and the urgency behind their work.

Learning is CUMULATIVE

It is on the basis of what they know and what they can do that pupils actively process new information they encounter and, as a consequence, derive new meanings.

'Teaching, whether through demonstration, explanation or asking questions, can only influence the course of intellectual development if the child is able to assimilate what is said and done.'

(Cobb et al, 1991)

This leads to a specific concept of learning called 'readiness', which holds out many implications for teachers as they design or choose resources or intervene in the students' learning.

Variety

You can use more than one activity in the main development stage if it suits your learning outcome. This will help with motivation, the hardest thing to maintain in a lesson. Another way of injecting variety is by using different resources such as a video clip followed by an information search on the internet and, finally, a written presentation using computers. Research suggests that students require 10-minute bursts in order to keep them on track – anything longer than 20 minutes and their learning appears to become less efficient.

Learning is INDIVIDUALLY DIFFERENT

The outcomes and processes of learning vary among students because of

'individual differences in the diversity of aptitudes that are relevant for learning, such as potential, prior knowledge, approaches to and conceptions of learning, interest, self-efficacy, self-worth and so on.'

(De Cortes, 1995)

Challenge

You must challenge students in class – through thought-provoking work their learning and understanding is more likely to be advanced. The challenge must be sufficient to make them think on a higher level, but not so high that they are unable to reach it due to lack of prior knowledge. When you are dealing with mixed ability classes this can be difficult – the easiest method is to provide the higher ability students with more open-ended activities that they can extend to meet their needs. However, even open-ended activities need to be well instructed to maintain the lesson outcome focus.

VAK – the learning styles

Visual, Audio, and Kinaesthetic/tactile are headings that describe particular types of learners. However, it must be made clear that we can all potentially be a combination of all three types of learning styles. Some of us will have a learning

Learning styles

Learning styles are conceptual, behavioural, cognitive, and effective patterns that are displayed over time and task.

National Curriulum in action

www.nc.action.org.uk

This is an excellent website for lesson design - specifically for getting ideas about different activities.

On the website you are able to search for examples of students' work under specific key stages and subjects.

style that suits us best - being aware of this will aid our learning as we understand what our ideal learning conditions are.

The Learning styles box (see page 57) describes some characteristics and strategies for learners.

So that's the theory, but how do you practically incorporate VAK into a lesson? Unless you are Superteacher you cannot possibly devise activities that combine the three learning styles every time. What you can do is try to mix up your activities so that sometimes they are more visual/auditory, e.g. watching TV and sometimes more kinaesthetic, e.g. making a mobile. With some activities it is good to provide students with a choice of how they go about the task, e.g. research through books or internet, etc, and they can then present their learning how they wish, e.g. poster or PowerPoint or radio interview.

A word of caution - it is important to challenge how our students learn. There is something to be said for occasionally placing them outside their comfort zone of learning. Even if you are a strongly visual learner there is nothing to say you cannot improve your audio or kinaesthetic skills - but you will only do this through practice.

Lesson plan templates

There are many templates that can be used when you have to produce a formal lesson plan - usually during your training year or during an inspection. Many schools have their own that they insist on their staff using. Other schools leave the lesson plan design up to the teacher. See the lesson plan template on page 59.

Learning styles

We are all different when it comes to how we like to learn but there seem to be three broad styles that people prefer.

Visual learners prefer:
- Information to be presented visually in written form
- Class notes, textbooks and summaries
- A quiet room for study

They can often see things in their mind's eye when trying to recall it.

Auditory learners prefer:
- Information presented in an oral form
- Class lectures and group work
- Interacting with others either by speaking or listening

They can often hear the way something was presented or rehearsed.

Kinaesthetic learners prefer:
- To be physically engaged in activities
- Class demonstrations and practical work
- To learn by experience

How does this apply to revision?

Visual learners
- Write out summary notes from class notes and textbooks
- Use flashcards
- Convert diagrams and charts into written notes, do the same for mathematical procedures
- Use Post-its for reminders
- Use colour coding to make things memorable

Auditory learners
- Make revision tapes to play to themselves
- Talk through mathematical procedures step by step
- Read revision notes out loud
- Join with others to revise

Kinaesthetic learners
- Walk about when revising and read information out loud
- Make models to illustrate concepts
- Make games and sorting tasks to give them something to do
- Copy information onto large pieces of paper using colourful pens
- Make revision tapes to listen to whilst exercising

Learning style survey

1. If I have to learn how to do something, I learn best when I:
(a) Watch someone show me how.
(b) Hear someone tell me how.
(c) Try to do it myself.

2. When I read, I often find that I:
(a) Visualise what I am reading in my mind's eye.
(b) Read out loud or hear the words inside my head.
(c) Fidget and try to 'feel' the content.

3. When asked to give directions, I:
(a) See the actual places in my head as I say them or prefer to draw them.
(b) Have no difficulty in giving them verbally.
(c) Have to point or move my body as I give them.

4. If I am unsure how to spell a word, I:
(a) Write it in order to see if it looks right.
(b) Spell it out loud in order to determine if it sounds right.
(c) Write it in order to see if it feels right.

5. When I write, I:
(a) Am concerned how neat and well spaced my letters and words appear.
(b) Often say the letters and words to myself.
(c) Push hard on my pen and can feel the flow of the words or letters as I form them.

6. If I had to remember a list of items, I would remember it best if I:
(a) Wrote them down.
(b) Said them over and over to myself.
(c) Moved around and used my fingers to name each item.

7. I prefer teachers who:
(a) Use the board or overhead projector while they lecture.
(b) Talk with a lot of expression.
(c) Use hands-on activities.

8. When trying to concentrate, I have a difficult time when:
(a) There is a lot of clutter or movement in the room.
(b) There is a lot of noise in the room.
(c) I have to sit still for any length of time.

9. When solving a problem, I:
(a) Write or draw diagrams to see it.
(b) Talk myself through it.
(c) Use my entire body or move objects to help me think.

10. When given instructions on how to build something, I:
(a) Read them silently and try to visualise how the parts will fit together.
(b) Read them out loud and talk to myself as I put the parts together.
(c) Try to put the parts together first then read later.

11. To keep occupied whilst waiting, I:
(a) Look around, stare, or read.
(b) Talk or listen to others.
(c) Walk around, manipulate things with my hands, or move/shake my feet as I sit.

12. If I had to verbally describe something to another person, I would:
(a) Be brief because I do not like to talk at length.
(b) Go into great detail because I like to talk.
(c) Gesture and move around while talking.

13. If someone was verbally describing something to me, I would:
(a) Try to visualise what she was saying.
(b) Enjoy listening but want to interrupt and talk myself.
(c) Become bored if her description got too long and detailed.

14. When trying to recall names, I remember:
(a) Faces but forget names.
(b) Names but forget faces.
(c) The situation that I met the person other than the person's name or face.

SCORING INSTRUCTIONS:
Add the number of responses for each letter and enter the total below. The area with the highest number of responses is probably your primary method of learning.

a = ...   Visual

b = ...   Auditory

c = ...   Kinaesthetic/tactile

Lesson plan template

LESSON PLAN

SUBJECT:

TOPIC:

YEAR GROUP: Year   **Pupil no:**   **Boys:**   **Girls:**

ABILITY:

SEN/G&T:

TEACHER:

DATE:

CONTEXT

Prior knowledge:

LEARNING OBJECTIVES

ACTIVITIES

Intro/starter activity: 0-15 mins

Main activity: 15-45 mins

Plenary: 45-60 mins

DIFFERENTIATION
- Pupils MUST...
- Pupils SHOULD...
- Pupils COULD...

ASSESSMENT
- Pupils' understanding assessed through...

HOMEWORK

Example of a lesson plan

LESSON PLAN

SUBJECT: Science KS3

TOPIC: LIGHT

YEAR GROUP: Year 8   **Pupil no:** 27   **Boys:** 16   **Girls:** 11

ABILITY: L – working at NC levels 3, 4 – a few approaching 5

SEN: BD, HP – statemented

Note: during this lesson both H and B are usually attending 'Successmaker' lessons. One to two LSAs are still present in this lesson.

TEACHER: LW

DATE: 3rd February 2007

CONTEXT

Third lesson in topic – Light – **NC ref:** 4.3 d *how light is refracted at the boundary between two different materials*

Prior knowledge:
a) *that light travels in a straight line at a finite speed in a uniform medium*
b) *that non-luminous objects are seen because light scattered from them enters the eye*
c) *how light is reflected at plane surfaces*

In summary: Pupils have previously investigated how the formation of shadows is an indication that light travels in straight lines. In their last lesson they investigated what happened to light as it was reflected from a mirror – leading to the relationship angle of incidence = angle of reflection.

LEARNING OBJECTIVES

1. To recall how light travels
2. To recall the relationship between the angle of incidence and the angle of reflection
3. To describe what happens to light when it 'hits' glass

ACTIVITIES

Intro/starter activity: 0–10 mins
→ On desk worksheet 1 *'How is light reflected from mirrors?'* – used to recall knowledge from previous lesson. The purpose of having work on their desk is twofold: first it ensures maximum learning time is used and secondly, provides an immediate task for even the most

distracted pupils to be doing as soon as they enter the classroom, i.e. no time available to chat.

Using PowerPoint
→ Give lesson objectives - setting the scene so that pupils understand what is expected and also a reference at the end of the lesson for what has been learnt.
→ Key words: refraction, bending, normal
→ 'What gets a reward stamp this lesson?' - reward system set up by the school for good work, behaviour etc.
→ 'Names in the bag' - a reward system used to encourage pupils to work hard in class - if the pupil's name stays in the bag for the duration of the lesson they are in the prize draw for a sweet - this means even if your name stays in you may not win the prize. Intermittent rewards are more successful than those that can always be achieved.

Main activity: 10-30 mins
→ Demo to pupils how to investigate what happens to light as it 'hits' glass using ray boxes.
→ Pupils carry out investigation using glass blocks and drawing ray diagrams in their books.
→ Discuss pupils' diagrams - *what has happened to light as it has passed through the glass and then out of the glass?*

Plenary: 30-45 mins
→ Show pictures of bending light diagrams - discuss why light bends through different substances using PowerPoint pictures of running through mud compared with running on roads - only level 5s may understand this!
→ Pupils to use worksheet 2 'Bending light - Refraction?' - to consolidate the ideas raised in the lesson re: that light bends as it passes through different mediums e.g. air to glass
→ Return to lesson objectives - have we achieved them?
→ Give out rewards.

DIFFERENTIATION
● Pupils MUST observe that light can bend as it passes from one medium to another.
● Pupils SHOULD be able to draw and label ray diagrams showing what happens to light as it passes from air to glass then glass to air.
● Pupils COULD begin to reason why light bends as it passes through different media.

ASSESSMENT
● Pupils' understanding assessed through worksheet 1 (intro) and 2 (plenary).
● Pupils' understanding assessed through discussion work and practical observations.
● Pupils who are working above level 4 given extension opportunities using worksheet 1.

HOMEWORK
Set on Wednesdays

Summary

✔ Use the National Curriculum/Specification to check exactly what it is that the students need to learn.

✔ Give yourself a break! Learn what they need to know first – if you have time learn additional information. Your knowledge will develop as you keep refreshing the same lesson.

✔ Don't be embarrassed to ask colleagues to explain something you can't get your head around. We've all been there – you can't be expected to know everything but you can be expected to find out!

✔ Add Pace, Variety and Challenge to your lesson activities.

✔ Be aware of which learning styles your activities provide – mix up these activities so that they suit all learners.

✔ Use a range of resources to add variety but ensure you allow students to interact with the resource.

✔ Use a standard lesson template to guide your planning.

Further activity

1. Practise planning for different learning styles by taking a single lesson objective and devising different activities that may favour:

   a. a visual learner

   b. an auditory learner

   c. a kinaesthetic learner.

2. Try to plan a single lesson: use the lesson format given in the chapter and take a single lesson objective. Break the objective up into starter, main and plenary activities. If you are stuck for lesson objectives, use a statement from the National Curriculum.

Chapter 6

Main Development Stage - Part 2

What will I learn in this chapter?

✔ How to use a lesson plan template

✔ How to choose the best resources in the classroom

✔ How to implement successful teaching strategies with individual resources

Resources and activities

Many things have changed since blackboards and chalk revolutionised the classroom. The modern teacher now has an array of resources to choose from. The great thing about having a choice is that if you mix up the resources you use in class you will help to keep your students focused as they change tack and learn from/through a different medium. Different resources also require different learning styles to be favoured. But which resource should you use to teach a specific learning point? In the first instance - whichever resource is most easily accessible. Over time your repertoire of resources will increase but for now choose good but simple resources - do vary it though. Most learning points are easily covered by a worksheet but try to vary this as many students are turned off by the constant filling in of worksheets and of glueing them into their books/files.

Resource media in the classroom

Do not succumb to the latest innovation! Yes, ICT (Information and Computer Technology) applications have their advantages - mainly that a task is often quicker or more efficient. However, like all resources they have a novelty factor attached. Mix up the resources you use in class so that the students are using a variety of skills.

Do remember that whatever resource you use, how you implement it in the classroom is the key to its success.

Worksheets

Worksheets come in all shapes and sizes and can contain a variety of activities. The most common worksheet will have some prose followed by some questions on the text just read. Others contain text with missing key words (gap fills) - very useful for checking students' understanding.

The advantages: easily produced and administered; useful for low ability students as they can save time writing; and appear better in books than some students' handwriting. The disadvantages: a wasteful resource, especially when you glue them into books on top of blank pages; and do not encourage students to write for themselves.

If you have a computer/OHP, project the worksheet onto the screen and get students to read from it (check for students with reading difficulties first) before answering questions or filling gaps in sentences. Some schools have very tight budgets on photocopying so 30 copies of worksheets are not popular. If something is best presented as a worksheet it may be worth laminating it so that although the initial cost is high it can be used over and over again.

A futuristic note: if Bill Gates' and other ICT advocates' future is realised, schools will be paper free with all students' work being produced on computers in a virtual learning environment. Actually many schools are already using this system in areas such as e-GCSEs where all the work is done on computers and sent off electronically for marking.

Practical elements

Many subjects have a practical element to them which is favoured by kinaesthetic learners. Practical subjects have the advantage of getting the students mobile and active whilst learning and for many this is fun. However, the downside of practical subjects is that they often take more preparation time, e.g. science, and can be more difficult to manage behaviour in. Therefore, practical activities must be well prepared and controlled from start to finish.

8 top tips for practical success

1. Go through and agree the rules of practical work before the activity so that you have made it perfectly clear what the consequences are for specific behaviour. Put the rules up on your wall so you can refer to them when necessary.

2. Ensure you have enough resources so that students are not fighting over one glue stick and a pair of scissors. Also, don't let them work in too big a group because you will have bystanders to the activity.

3. If you have a seating plan, don't let it change in practical work. If students are sitting in pairs let them do the practical work as the same pair.

4. Carefully lay out the room so that students are spread out and are working safely.

5. Spread out resources – use resource trays or boxes. This will prevent students from all gathering in one part of the room.

6. Make sure all belongings are placed away from the work area so that students are not distracted. Do this in all lessons but particularly in practical sessions.

7. Periodically stop the students and check where they are so that you can maintain the pace - give time checks.

8. Don't be afraid to prevent a student from doing practical work if they have shown dangerous behaviour - agree with another class teacher that you can send individuals to them if necessary. Do let students redeem themselves next lesson by allowing them to show that they can do the work safely.

Text

Textbooks still seem to be the most prevalent resource used in the classroom. Teachers and students still spend much of their educational resource budget on this learning tool. This is not to say that ICT does not provide an alternative but for now textbooks' accessibility and availability to all appears to be the winning factor in terms of resource choice.

So how best to use texts? For a start, carefully choose a textbook that matches your students' needs - make sure it has the correct reading age and covers the content being studied. The book must be student friendly - use of colour and broken-up text helps. How the text is laid out can put some students off from the beginning or, likewise, motivate them to read on.

Do you read as a class or allow students to read individually? Again, mix it up - both methods are useful. Reading as a class allows individuals to read out loud to an audience whilst the others learn to follow the text and listen patiently. Reading individually allows students to read at their own pace. Sometimes both methods can be incorporated as you encourage students to read text twice to give them a better understanding.

Reward students who volunteer to read or alternatively inform students you will choose them randomly as the text is read - the latter method encourages students to follow the text as peers read just in case they are next and need to know where to start reading from. Do be sensitive to weak readers - don't avoid them but give them easy sections to read or smaller ones so as to include and encourage them.

TV and video/DVDs

TV and its applications are often used as a reward at the end of the day or year but it is a resource that, when applied appropriately, can help with the understanding of concepts that have a visual element to them, e.g. global warming.

TV use in the classroom

Don't feel students have to huddle round the front of a TV. Keep them in their seats (as long as they can see). This will help maintain focus and behaviour.

Don't feel you have to show an entire film when only two minutes is appropriate. Just show what's needed and move on – this is easier when using DVDs on computers rather than TV.

There is a large selection of videos/DVDs available – so choose well! As with the textbook, you need to aim for the correct age/content and features that will keep the students watching. Do watch the video/DVD before the lesson so that you know for certain that it is appropriate and go on colleagues' recommendations.

Very rarely is it appropriate to show a video/DVD without some interaction alongside, unless it is very short and even then it is best to give students a focus for their viewing. This focus maybe a simple question.

ICT

As each academic year passes more and more money is pouring into ICT resources. This is partly due to the government push to provide all students with computer access in order to learn the basic workforce ICT skills required to compete in the global market. Interestingly, most of this money has simply gone into resources and not training. The lack of training has led to an inefficient usage of ICT in most schools lucky enough to have these modern tools. If you are fortunate enough to have ICT facilities available to you, use them. But, like any other resource, don't over-rely on them. Remember, variety is good!

TEACHING TIPS

Common strategies for optimising students' learning experience when using resources

✔ Support students in selecting information.

✔ Encourage active participation.

✔ Ensure the resource allows the student to work at an appropriate level.

✔ Allow students *some* control over their learning.

✔ Encourage learning-conducive interaction between students.

Common ICT applications

1. **PowerPoint** – great for quick access to text, pictures and video. Saves writing on a board and allows you to import different learning tools to enhance the students' learning.

2. **Interactive boards** – great for allowing students to get involved with their learning by moving objects around, writing, drawing, etc, all of which can be

saved. There are some very good programs for all key stages in most subjects which provide the teacher with a good stock of lessons.

Due to the cost of interactive boards many schools have opted for data projectors (you can get six data projectors to one board). However, you can still use interactive material on your screen by just using the mouse on your keyboard instead of a pen.

3. **Internet** – a great source of information – but make sure you structure this use as it is quite a skill to use search engines well and get specific information. 'WebQuests' are becoming more common – these are specific web pages that contain tasks with links to useful websites.

4. **DVDs/CD-roms** - in time DVDs played on computers will surpass videos on TVs just because of the ease of use and ability to skip scenes quickly – making lesson and learning time more efficient.

You should make a point of using ICT in your teaching simply because of its time-saving ability. Lessons can be written and saved for next year or changed and updated. Lessons can flow seamlessly as you can use video, audio and interactive formats from one resource. Many new schemes of work are available online with PowerPoint lessons available. However, don't become too lazy – even the best content needs to be adapted for the needs of your own class.

Using technology in the classroom

www.curriculumonline.gov.uk provides teachers with guidance on how to use specific technology in the classroom. The website also provides specific ideas for key stage/subject use.

The website includes case studies from teachers. These are always useful as you know that what is being suggested has been tried and tested.

Importantly, teachers must use more and more ICT in schools to complement the emerging technologies that the students themselves are using out of school – this includes the use of mobile phones. Check your school policy: students are often allowed to have mobiles in school but not to use them. This is a shame really – they have many uses.

Use a mobile phone to:

- Calculate.
- Capture photos of activities – many phones allow you to download this information onto computers.
- Record video.

Use a digital camera to:

- Capture information in stills – great for drama.

- Add to a recipe or practical investigation – each step is put in words and a picture.

- Replace class rules with pictures of positive behaviour.

- Take on trips to use as evidence of activities – 'What did you see?' Then when you return to the classroom the students can go through their pictures to describe their experience – a bit like showing your holiday pictures.

- Encourage pupils to take pictures about their and others' lives, their community, etc; great for PSHE (Personal, Social and Health Education)/citizenship studies.

- Make artwork.

Use digital video

The same activities as with the camera, but using moving images. Show students how to edit their film using packages like Windows Media. By editing their work students can become increasingly critical of what was more and less important in their films.

Free IT resources

Futurelab is an educational charity that has produced several IT applications for schools to use in the classroom – including the award-winning Create-A-Scape where students interact in a virtual environment. Many applications are free to download.

www.futurelab.org.uk

Students know how to use these technologies and like using them, so why not use them in the classroom? Don't be afraid of ICT – try to embrace it. Just get guidance from colleagues who are more familiar with such tools, then practise – it will be worth it. Alternatively, find out which students are particularly good with ICT and get them to help you plan and implement the lesson – let them be the expert and acknowledge this fact. As teachers we cannot be expected to know and do everything, but we can encourage students to share their own skills and to celebrate this with them.

Summary

✔ Think before choosing your resource – is it the best one to deliver a specific learning objective?

✔ Think carefully about which strategies you will use alongside your chosen resource. Ensure that the students are not passive learners.

✔ Do embrace technology – bring into your lesson technologies the students use out of the classroom.

✔ Allow students who are good with ICT to lead lessons or even help you plan lessons involving such tools.

Further activity

1. Use your mobile phone to explore activities you may be able to use it for in the classroom.

2. Start recording TV programmes that may contain useful clips to use in your lesson.

Chapter 7

Plenary Work

What will I learn in this chapter?

✔ How to plan a good plenary

✔ How to assess learning through plenary work

✔ Examples of plenaries

How do you know what your students have learnt during a lesson? How do you know how much an individual has taken in and what misconceptions they may still hold? Teachers cannot take it for granted that if all 30 students have completed the tasks put in front of them they have fully understood the knowledge and concepts presented during the lesson. It is very easy for a student to hide behind their peers and appear to have learnt everything – until faced with test results.

Give advance warning

Inform your students at the start of the lesson what the plenary activity will be. This will allow the students time to think and plan the activity. Be clear about what you expect to see or hear. Keep reminding them of this task during the lesson.

Often this plenary will be in the form of a presentation where the students explain or show what they have learnt and can discuss what they struggled with or found easy – refer to notes on metacognition.

The plenary is not simply a summary of the lesson's main learning points – it is a useful activity in itself. The purpose of a plenary is to assess your students' overall learning for the lesson so that you can reflect on this afterwards and plan your next class appropriately, with any intervention work for individuals if deemed necessary.

Debriefing during the plenary – Fisher, 2001

Debriefing is an important part of a plenary – it is where you discuss what has been learnt. Fisher (2001) identified three intentions of the debrief:

1. Ask students to give answers and explain how they reached them.
2. Encourage students to use the appropriate language when explaining.
3. Encourage students to think how this new knowledge or skill can be transferred to another area. This is often referred to as 'bridging'.

So how do you assess what students have learnt?

The format of a plenary can take the general form shown below:

1. Remind students of lesson objectives.

2. Carry out an activity that checks their learning – see box for examples.

3. Use traffic light cards to show overall learning. This can be done by asking students to hold up the colour that best matches their understanding of each objective. This is not perfect but will give you an overall snapshot.

4. Inform students what they will be moving on to next lesson, i.e. make links between lessons so they do not see them as one-off learning events.

Although the above is the general format for a good plenary it is important that you add variety by using different activities to assess students' learning at Stage 2.

An example of a 10-minute plenary

- Return to the lesson objectives and remind students what they are meant to have learnt.

- Provide students with mini whiteboards and pens.

- Ask five questions that cover today's work and get students to write answers on whiteboards.

- Ask students to share their answers – each time pointing out which lesson objective they are showing knowledge of.

- Provide students with traffic light cards (red, amber and green – helpful if schools place these in student planners). Ask students to assess their own learning by showing the colour that best represents their understanding of a particular objective.

So how long should you spend on a plenary? As a rule 10 minutes minimum should be plenary-type activities in an hour lesson. In practice this part of the lesson suffers mostly due to mistimings earlier on – to the point that it is not unusual for teachers to miss it out completely. However, even if you know an activity in the main development stage is running over time it is better to cut that short and assess what has been learnt than to continue the activity and not assess at all. The reason for this is that you need to know for planning for the next lesson what learning has or has not occurred. If you have a double lesson it is best to split it into two halves with two plenaries. This last method also helps maintain student motivation if they know they have already made learning gains.

Interacting with the whole class

Whole class interaction has been shown to be very successful in raising attainment.

One such study showed that 'effective teachers' tended to teach the whole class actively, spending significantly more time than ineffective teachers lecturing, demonstrating or interacting with the class (Rosenshine, 1979).

Use everything in your teaching repertoire - provide the students with a mix. Lecturing may appear old fashioned but it has its place alongside inquiry learning and collaborative learning.

Olson and Torrance (1998) recognised that teachers need to deploy a range of different pedagogic approaches and teaching strategies to meet the needs of the subject, to meet the objective and to match the age and ability of the students.

Examples of plenary activities

All the activities used as starters can be adapted to be used in the plenary (see Chapter 4); however, the activities below are particularly good for this stage of the lesson.

'Who Wants to be a Millionaire?'

Again a TV quiz show comes to the rescue. If it can attract audiences into the millions why not use it in class? Students are familiar with the format of top game shows so feel comfortable playing them. Do not worry what colleagues think - as long as you are using the game as a learning activity then you are justified in doing so.

'Who Wants to be a Millionaire?' can be played using an ICT program or cards. They both follow the same principles of design - it just tends to be quicker using ICT. Simply make up a question with four possible answers - either read out the options A to D or show the questions and answers on the board. Make up cards with the letters A to D on them and tie them together with a tag. Hand a pack out to each student. As you ask or show each question all the students show a card. Again this is a good exercise in allowing you to get a snapshot of what the whole class has learnt. To add excitement you can follow the game show and allow them three lifelines - ask a friend, ask the whole class or 50:50.

Best of Five

We all get stuck on what to do for a plenary occasionally or simply run out of time to properly implement the one we had planned to use. A good 'get out of jail' activity is Best of Five - here you simply pick on individuals to answer a question correctly. The aim of the game is for the class to answer five questions in a row correctly.

Test paper questions

Many would say that giving students a past paper question to attempt as a plenary is the perfect way of assessing what they have learnt. Exam boards and QCA both produce materials for teachers in a range of subjects and key stages to use for assessment. Some of these materials are IT based and allow you to make up your own test from exam papers very quickly. Ask your school if they have or are willing to buy a program entitled 'Test Base' (QCA) - it's well worth it. Alternatively, you can buy exam papers and do a cut and paste but obviously this takes much longer.

Odd One Out

Similar to 'Who Wants to be a Millionaire?', Odd One Out is a series of questions with three or four answers but with one of them incorrect.

English KS3/4

Which of the following characters did not appear in Shakespeare's play 'Macbeth'?

A. Duncan   **B. Edward**
C. Hecate   D. Malcolm

Maths KS2

Which of the following numbers is not a prime number?

1   11   **22**   57

Pass the Bag

In a bag place some questions based on the lesson. Play some music whilst the students pass around the bag, when you pause the music the student with the bag has to pick out a question and answer it – if they get it correct they are next in line to leave the classroom when the bell goes. This is a good technique to use on classes that have individuals always in a rush to get out. Alternatively, place a word, number, date, name, etc in the bag and ask the students to form a question for the class so they can guess what was on the card.

Metacognition

Put simply, metacognition is thinking about thinking. It is the process where students take conscious control of their learning. The learner thinks about how they are thinking. For example, the learner is using metacognition if they realise that they are having more trouble learning how to complete a fraction problem than a multiplication problem.

Examples of metacognitive questions:

- What did you think was easy to do and what did you think was hard to do?
- What changes would you wish to make?
- What is the most important thing you learned from this?
- What do you do when you find something difficult?

These questions are useful at the plenary stage of a lesson as they allow the student to reflect on their learning and what they could do to make further improvements.

Five Ws

This encourages students to ask their own questions and to consider the different types of questions and the individual responses they bring with them. The Five Ws are *Who, What, Where, When* and *Why*. Once they have devised their questions they can pass them on to another student or pair to answer. Alternatively, this activity can be carried out as a whole class.

With all these activities what we are trying to do is motivate the students to carry out a task whilst learning at the same time.

Planning and student behaviour

'Effective teachers experience fewer problems with ending the lesson than less effective teachers, through methods such as planning and pacing the lesson to leave sufficient time for activities at the end of the lesson.'

(Muijs and Reynolds, 2001)

Summary

✔ A good plenary will assess how much learning has occurred.

✔ Refer to learning objectives when assessing learning.

✔ Give advance warning of the plenary so students know what they are aiming for.

✔ Spend at least 10 minutes on the plenary.

✔ Inform students how what they have learnt will link to next lesson.

Further activity

Buy some green, orange, red card from a stationers (or from your school) and make up 30 sets of traffic light cards.

Make up 30 sets of cards with A, B, C, D written on alternate sides.

Both these sets of resources will be invaluable when delivering plenaries.

Chapter 8

Managing Behaviour through Lesson Planning

What will I learn in this chapter?

✔ How to install good behaviour management through lesson planning

✔ How to model good behaviour

✔ The use of rewards and positive language in the classroom

'I am the decisive element in the classroom. It is my personal approach that creates the climate. It is my daily mood that makes the weather. As a teacher I possess tremendous power to make a child's life miserable or joyous. I can be a tool of torture or an inspiration. I can humble or humour, hurt or heal. In all sets it is my response that decides whether a crisis will be exacerbated or de-escalated – a child humanised or de-humanised.'

(Haim Ginott, 1972)

Many schools have separate teaching and learning and behaviour management policies. However, a few recognise that successful teaching and learning frameworks make having a separate policy for behaviour redundant as they deal implicitly with behavioural issues. The idea is that if you provide a good curriculum and lessons are thoughtfully planned with individuals in mind then the majority of students will behave well, as they will be engaged with their learning. Many schools have added to their teaching and learning policy a section called Behaviour for Learning, making specific links between behaviour and learning – see box. In practice both methods are workable – the key to any school managing behaviour well is that there is a policy that provides guidelines and that staff consistently adhere to it. Even a weak behaviour policy will be more successful than a well thought out one if all the staff buy into it. One of the biggest gripes within the profession is how some colleagues ignore behaviour and at best just pass it on to someone else to deal with. If you want to be respected by students you must work with the school and carry out its policy, however weak it may appear. If you are concerned by the policy join a working party that has influence on it or write to the Head with your concerns and suggestions. Try not to become a teacher who sits in the staff-room moaning about behaviour when you do not follow through on school sanctions or ignore poor behaviour. Students are clever – they soon work out which teachers will pull them up

Causes of poor behaviour

Croll and Moses (2000) suggested that teachers feel that 80% of challenging behaviour is caused by problems 'within the child' or 'home'. However, Beaman and Wheldall (2000) found that:

'On-task behaviour of the same students varies across subjects and teachers.

When teachers increase the number of positive verbal interventions, there is an increase in the level of students' on-task behaviour.'

and follow through with consequences and which ones will not bother. The issue of behaviour is hard to begin with as students get to know you and many will naturally challenge you, but I promise you in the long run dealing with poor behaviour is worth the effort!

The golden rule

You need to be careful in not overdoing the rules. A useful rule I kept on my board read: *'The golden rule is . . . we always listen to one another in silence.'* If the rule was being broken I would point to the board and wait until the behaviour changed.

Behaviour for learning

✔ Arrive on time, fully equipped and ready to get to work immediately.

✔ Sit where you are told to sit and stay seated.

✔ Put up your hand and wait to be asked to speak.

✔ Listen in silence when another person or your teacher is speaking.

✔ Respect one another's efforts and achievements.

✔ Work hard without distracting others.

✔ Drink water only – to keep you alert in class.

✔ Pack up your belongings when instructed to do so.

Giving the right impression

As soon as you walk through the school gates you set an impression – you need to make sure it's the right one. If you see students, acknowledge them – say, 'Good morning' – and go on your way. As you get to know students better you may have more of a conversation but what you are doing here is modelling manners.

Be on time for lessons. As mentioned in Chapter 1, students will soon learn that you are always in your class on time and that shows them two things: first, you take this teaching and learning stuff seriously and second, you are modelling the

importance of good timekeeping. If you are occasionally late always apologise to them and briefly explain why – again you are modelling behaviour you expect from the students who come in late.

Plan your lessons well. You can't get away from the simple fact that if you plan and deliver a good lesson the students know you are putting time into their learning and should respect you for that. However much fun students appear to have in an unplanned and unruly lesson, they usually get bored of this and start complaining. At the end of the day most if not all students want to learn and achieve; if you have planned a lesson and behaviour is still poor it could be that it was too difficult. Students must feel challenged by the learning in class but the learning must also be achievable – this is a hard one to judge but as you get to know your classes you will learn the level they engage at.

Mark homework. Keeping on top of your marking can have a significant impact in helping to maintain good relationships with your classes. Students appreciate that you have taken time to do this work and that you are in touch with an area of their studies that many teachers find difficult to keep up with. Students will take you more seriously because you know how they are progressing in class and at home. Importantly, it allows you to intervene early on – whether just with the student or with the Tutor/Head of Year or with parents. But how do you keep on top of homework? First you set yourself a realistic goal – you can't mark every single piece of weekly homework for a start, neither can you not set regular homework as you will no doubt have a homework policy. You do not need to mark every piece yourself – homework is great for self- and peer-assessment opportunities – the important thing is that you at least acknowledge those who have spent time doing homework (this can be part of your register). See Chapter 12 for guidance.

Modelling behaviour – Bandura, 1977

The social learning theory of Bandura emphasises the importance of observing and modelling the behaviours, attitudes, and emotional reactions of others.

'Learning would be exceedingly laborious, not to mention hazardous, if people had to rely solely on the effects of their own actions to inform them what to do. Fortunately, most human behaviour is learned observationally through modelling: from observing others one forms an idea of how new behaviours are performed, and on later occasions this coded information serves as a guide for action.' (p 22)

Actions Bring Consequences

Many schools and specifically referral units have embraced the behaviour model 'Actions Bring Consequences' or 'The ABC of Behaviour'. The idea is that we all have to take responsibility for our **actions** and accept the **consequences** if we make inappropriate choices about how to behave. The system is designed to warn students when they are misbehaving that there will be a **consequence** if they **choose** to continue. The aim is to help students to develop **self-discipline** and avoid negative **consequences**. This is an essential 'Behaviour for Learning *and* Life'. Students who **choose** to follow the classroom rules and get on with their learning receive a positive **consequence** in the form of praise and reward.

Avoiding confrontation

✔ Use appropriate language.

✔ Maintain mutual respect.

✔ Safeguard the student's sense of self.

✔ Finish discussion on a positive note or expectation, e.g. 'I know you can do this . . .'

✔ Give students take-up time. If they are angry or frustrated they will not be able to turn round their behaviour straight away.

Two very important aspects of 'Actions Bring Consequences' to remind students of

1. **It is totally unacceptable to disrupt a lesson because it stops other students learning.** If students ignore how their behaviour affects others around them they can expect a consequence because they have interfered with other students' right to learn.

2. **It is totally unacceptable to argue with your teacher or question their decision because it disrupts the lesson and is disrespectful to your teacher.**

   'Do what you are asked to do the first time and do not argue at the point of the incident!'

It is important to convey the idea that there are positive as well as negative consequences to our actions. Schools often use the symbols below to illustrate this.

- Positive consequences, called **'Ps'** ('Praises')
- Negative consequences in the classroom, called **'Cs'**
- Negative consequences for out of lesson behaviour, called **COs**

If this system is working well your school should have at least a 1:3 ratio of Cs to Ps – demonstrating that rewarding good behaviour helps rein in poor behaviour.

Have a sense of humour

Students respond well to humour. If done well it can help to redirect a student or group. Never use sarcasm, they won't like it!

Top strategies for managing behaviour

✔ Tactically ignore poor behaviour – not all instances but insignificant ones

✔ Use simple, brief directional statements or rule reminders

✔ Give non-verbal, non-confrontational messages

✔ Use direct rule statements – expect compliance

✔ Use 'when' . . . 'then' directions

✔ Use casual questions to refocus

✔ Give realistic choices, reminding students of the consequences system

✔ Use 'Thanks' rather than 'Please'

✔ Give take-up time – don't expect an immediate turnaround. Walk away – this gives the impression that the change in behaviour is expected. Do not stare at a student waiting for the change – you'll wind them up!

✔ Model behaviour you wish to see

✔ Protect the students' self-esteem

✔ Catch them being good!

Language for learning

Useful phrases to encourage students who are struggling with a task:

'I know you can . . . '

'You can do it. What help do you need?'

'This is difficult . . . which bit can't you do yet?'

'When you finish . . . '

'Which part did I not explain well enough?'

'I'm sorry, I should have made it clearer.'

Reconciliation meetings

The rationale behind reconciliation meetings is that they help you to re-establish a working relationship with a student you may have had an incident with in a lesson or, equally as important, out of lesson time.

Reconciliation meetings

These meetings can make all the difference. It is important that if a student has been sent out of a lesson you catch up with them prior to the next one. Otherwise, you may face a confrontation right from the start of your next lesson. Importantly, you and the student will feel much better about the next time you meet and not dread it.

Ask the teacher to whom you have sent the student to keep them behind so that you can pop in at the end and arrange a time to reconcile (unless it is break or lunch time). Write this appointment in their journal as a record.

How to have a successful reconciliation meeting – see Chapter 8.

Tips for reconciliation meetings

- Thank the student for staying back
- Tune in to how they are feeling
- Focus on specific behaviour observed
- Relate behaviour to consequences system
- Invite feedback

- Ask them to consider what they might do instead of this behaviour
- State expectation and confidence for next time
- Part amicably

Rewards systems

There are many rewards systems that both schools and individual teachers use successfully. The important thing is that you have a rewards system and that you use it.

TEACHING TIPS

How to use praise

Praise is best received when:

✔ It is personal - use students' names.

✔ It is genuine.

✔ It is appropriate - don't be flippant with praise otherwise it will lose its currency.

✔ It is specific - explain what it is for, this will help the student to repeat the behaviour.

✔ It is consistent.

✔ It is used regularly.

Ace cards are an example of a rewards system that can be used by an individual teacher, a faculty, a year group or a whole school. They simply work by handing out laminated cards to students who have made a significant achievement in a lesson, for the term or year, or out of school. Each Ace card is then placed in a raffle with the student's name on it - raffles are then carried out (great in assemblies) and an appropriate prize given. Prizes can be contentious, with many staff believing student's should be motivated by results alone. However, the reality is rewards are received very well and do not have to be over the top. Some schools hand out learning equipment/school bags/sportsgear and others build up to bigger raffles with mountain bikes being won! You would be amazed how many local businesses will give out donations - it's worth asking as school budgets don't extend to prizes.

Non-verbal ways of giving praise

✔ Smiling – helps maintain the wanted behaviour.

✔ Nodding to affirm or approve.

✔ 'Thumbs up' to acknowledge achievement.

✔ 'Soft' applause to congratulate.

✔ Mouthing to show delight.

Example of a school's rewards system

All students at St Katherine's will be rewarded for high attendance, good effort and good behaviour.

In class you can gain rewards in the form of praises (Ps). Praises will be recorded as follows:

Verbal	P1
Stamp	P2
Praise postcard	P3
Formal letter from teacher/tutor	P4
Formal letter from Head of Faculty or Head of Year	P5
Good progress check or report letter from a Senior Teacher	P10

Documenting incidents/phone calls

Get a diary, a large one – say A4 size with a day to each page. Then use this to document not only lessons and perhaps their titles but also meetings/events and any incidents or phone calls that have occurred that day. The reason for this is that it is useful to have a record of events so that when you talk to a parent, students or Head of Year you can be clear on what you did and what you said. You don't have to write an essay, just the key points.

Summary

✔ Give the students the right impression – be fair and consistent as you adhere to the school's policy on behaviour.

✔ Be on time for lessons.

✔ Mark or acknowledge all homework.

✔ Teach the students that 'Actions Bring Consequences' and that these consequences can be both positive and negative.

✔ You need to be giving out at least a 1:3 ratio of negative to positive consequences.

✔ Use reconciliation meetings to work out issues with individuals before the next lesson.

✔ Ensure the students know the rules and that you will adhere to them.

✔ Avoid confrontations by using a language of choice.

✔ Have a sense of humour but do not use sarcasm.

✔ Contact parents to inform them of both negative and positive incidents – get them on your side by keeping them informed of their child's development.

✔ Keep a record of all contacts with parents – get a large diary!

Further activity

1. Buy a large A4 diary to record phone calls/important events.

2. Get hold of a large mark book and plan out how you are to record the following (highlighter pens are very useful):

   SEN codes

   G&T

   Action plan codes

   Homework set/completed

   Praise awarded

   Baseline data, i.e. the students' grade/level they are currently at and what they are working towards by the end of their key stage.

   (Note: baseline data should be given to you with your class lists at the start of the year.)

3. Find out about the learning difficulties associated with: Asperger's Syndrome, Dyspraxia, Dyslexia, Fragile X, ADHD, Oppositional Defiant Disorder.

Chapter 9

Literacy and Numeracy

What will I learn in this chapter?

✔ How to promote literacy and numeracy skills in every lesson

✔ How to plan for individual learning needs

✔ How to further the learning of the gifted and talented

✔ How to effectively use LSAs in the classroom

As teachers of any subject or key stage we are expected to build literacy and numeracy opportunities into our lessons wherever possible. Obviously if you are a maths or English teacher part of this chapter may appear redundant. If you are a primary school teacher you will need to formally spend time on these two disciplines daily. However, if you are teaching a subject or topic that does not appear to naturally lend itself to literacy and numeracy activities – think again.

Literacy

Key words

All topics and subjects can have key words highlighted. Students benefit from focusing on these in lessons. Key words may be technical words or expressive words depending on the subject and task at hand.

Key words are best introduced with learning objectives at the start of a lesson. However, be careful not to give out too many key words – this can be very daunting. Four or five should be ample – fewer for weaker students. During the lesson encourage students to use these words in their spoken and written work. Congratulate students when they use a key word with positive reinforcement.

If you have time, during a topic make card cutouts of key words and place around the room as a constant reminder to the students. Alternatively, write the key words on your board and leave them for the duration of the lesson so that you can point to them if necessary.

TEACHING TIPS

Mnemonics

A mnemonic is a device that aids the memorisation of something:

● Rhymes.

● Acronyms.

e.g. **M**onkey **N**ot **E**ating **M**eans **O**ld **N**utshells **I**n **C**arpet

Ask students to make up their own mnemonics for key words. Great to help with spelling or an order:

'**M**y **V**ery **E**asy **M**ethod – **J**ust **S**et **U**p **N**ine **P**lanets'

Mercury, Venus, Earth, Mars, Jupiter, Saturn, Uranus, Neptune, Pluto

Writing frames

Writing frames are very useful and can be used with the full spectrum of students' ability. They help train the students on how to present an idea or how to express their thoughts. In particular, when working with groups who have low motivation and hate writing, they can be useful as they cut down writing and make it easier for students to complete the task – focusing on the key learning points.

An example of a writing frame to help students develop explanations

There are differing explanations as to Why (How, What, When, etc)

One explanation is that ....

The evidence for this is ....

An alternative explanation is ....

This explanation is based on ....

Of the alternative explanations I think the most likely is ....

Sentence frames

A sentence frame is just a simplified version of a writing frame. Once again they help students express themselves by showing how a sentence may be constructed.

Examples of a sentence frame

'I predict .... will happen because........ .'

'I would describe John as .... : this is because ....'

'I think ....because ....'

Modelling

This is a very effective method of introducing students to the conventions of text. The teacher shows how to construct a new text/answer by expressing their thinking out loud.

Using good and bad responses to questions or examples of text is useful for eliciting conventions.

Providing students with model answers is useful for all ages and levels.

Presentations – speaking

Many students wince at the thought of standing up in front of their peers and speaking. To make this easier put shy students with more confident ones so they can have a safety net of sorts. However, make it clear that they both need to participate. Mixing pairs will help the weaker student develop as they learn from their partner. Let gifted and talented students or those who are confident speakers present alone.

Presentations need structuring – so give students a framework to use. The framework could be a series of questions they have found the answers to and are using to simply feed back their findings.

If available, allow students to present using applications such as PowerPoint – this will give them an aid and make them feel more confident. It is also a useful exercise as PowerPoint is now universally used in presentations. Alternatively, give out acetate sheets and OHP non-permanent pens and ask students to present using this aid on the overhead projector.

Discussions

Most good lessons have a discussion section simply because this is an effective method for the teacher to use in receiving feedback from the students – what do they already know and what have they learnt so far? Discussions also allow students to express their opinions and thoughts – the DCSF is keen for teachers to capture students' 'creativity' and help them develop this skill further.

USEFUL WEBSITE

Creativity

To find out more about the DCSF guidelines to creativity go to:

http://www.ncaction.org.uk/creativity/index.htm

Similar to progressive questioning, try to develop the discussion so that it progressively becomes more challenging.

Reading

Other than English teachers – who often have library lessons built into their timetable and of course primary school teachers who may adhere to the literacy hour – many teachers often shy away from reading in class thinking it is 'old fashioned'. However, reading is another activity that you can add to the mix to provide variety but also help students to develop this critical literacy skill. As mentioned in Chapter 5, reading can be performed in several ways in class.

- Read in silence
- Read as a class – students are chosen to read sections
- Have students read the text several times but ask them to interpret at a greater level each time. For example, highlight key words, use a dictionary to check understanding of key words, describe main points, summarise text in own words, link points to something they already know, etc

The important point is that you do not avoid opportunities for students to read – but to jazz it up make them more interactive with the text so they are demonstrating their learning and understanding.

Listening

As any teacher will tell you this is a skill many students find difficult. Funnily enough, reading as a class is often a time when students are silent and listening, especially if they know it could be their turn to read next. In fact, you generally find they are a lot better at listening to one another than they are to you. However, this is not always the case; good listening skills are part of good manners as well as a capability to allow students to learn effectively.

- Record radio material
- Use audio tapes – books/plays, etc
- Ask students to make their own recordings

Using audio material alone will narrow down the senses students can use to understand what is going on and will hopefully focus their attention on listening.

Assessment for learning – reflective work

As Chapter 11 will show, assessment for learning is an important classroom tool to allow students the time to reflect on what they already know, what they have learnt and how they can improve. This work can be done through peer discussion work where students talk to one another about their learning and what they may have found easy or difficult, then move on to discussing what they need to do next to improve. As a whole class you may ask some pairings to feed back from their discussions so that you and the others get an idea of where their learning is. This will help your planning for next lesson.

TEACHING TIPS

Interactive planning tools

You can access an Interactive Planning Tool for primary teaching from the website **www.standards.dfes.gov.uk**. This tool allows teachers to draw on the extensive resources and guidance currently available for literacy and mathematics. The tool enables teachers to incorporate this material into their own lesson plans and share it with colleagues.

Numeracy

TEACHING REFERENCE

Defining numeracy

'Numeracy is a proficiency which is developed mainly in maths but also in other subjects. It is more than an ability to do basic arithmetic. It involves confidence and competence with numbers and measures. It requires an understanding of the number system, a repertoire of mathematical techniques, and an inclination and ability to solve quantitative and spatial problems in a range of contexts. Numeracy also demands understanding of the ways in which data are gathered by counting and measuring, and presented in graphs, diagrams, charts and tables. Handling data is of particular relevance to all subjects.'

(DfEE, Framework for Teaching Mathematics, 2001,
see www.standards.dfes.gov.uk)

Problem-solving

Many topics have a problem-solving element to them. Problem-solving is a good exercise for students as it encourages independent thinking. Instead of students being spoon-fed facts and explanations, it provides them with evidence to use in order to solve problems. If students can learn to look at evidence critically and evaluate it to form a judgement or simply an answer then we are aiding their intellectual growth.

Calculations

Many questions can lead to a numerate answer in all topics/subjects.

- How long ago did ...... happen?
- How old would ...... be if he were alive today?
- What is the difference between the ages of the two characters?
- How long will it take before .... happens?
- If the time is ...... and the buns take .... minutes to bake, when will they be ready?

Graphing

Timelines, as well as more traditional graphs such as pie charts and histograms, are very useful in representing information neatly, particularly in presentations. Encourage students to use them by presenting information to them on a graph and asking them to interpret what it shows.

TEACHING TIPS

Using graphs for storytelling

In English ask students to draw a graph showing the mood or intensity of the story as it proceeds.

In History use graphs to report events.

This device can work in both directions, i.e. you draw the graph and they interpret, or they draw the graph from the story or event.

Summary

✔ Take any opportunity to practise literacy and numeracy skills in your lessons.

✔ Use key words, writing frames, sentence frames, presentations and discussion work to practise literacy.

✔ Use problem-solving, calculations and graph work to practise numeracy.

✔ As schools become more inclusive (see Chapter 10) you must plan for individual needs.

Further activity

Make up key word cards for numeracy and literacy skills often covered at your key stage or in your subject. See the QCA SOW for guidance at **www.qca.org.uk**

Chapter 10

Special Educational Needs and Gifted and Talented

What will I learn in this chapter?

✔ How to manage students with Individual Education Plans/ Statements

✔ How to use LSAs effectively in the classroom

✔ How to challenge gifted and talented students

✔ How to employ the personalised learning agenda in lesson planning

Inclusion and Special Educational Needs

During the 1980s and 1990s there was much investment put into setting up 'Special Schools' to meet the needs of individuals with learning or physical difficulties. However, since the start of the 21st century there has been a shift in thinking with many special schools closing or merging with their nearest secondary school. The rationale behind this latest philosophical shift is that the social aspect of schooling is crucial to all students and that whatever a student's learning or physical ability, most if not all their needs are best met in an inclusive social environment. Many secondary schools now have separate Inclusion teams or faculties to meet the change in student profile.

Statutory obligation

The National Curriculum 2000 gives statutory guidance on inclusion, requiring teachers to:

- Set suitable learning challenges.
- Respond to students' diverse leaning needs.
- Overcome potential barriers to learning.

What is inclusive teaching?

'An educationally inclusive school is one in which the teaching and learning, achievements, attitudes and the well-being of every young person matter. This shows not only in their performance, but also in the ethos and willingness to offer new opportunities to pupils who may have experienced previous difficulties. This does not mean treating all pupils in the same way, rather it involves taking account of pupils' varied life experiences and needs.'

(Evaluating Educational Inclusion, www.ofsted.gov.uk)

Individual Education Plans (IEPs)/Statements

Many students in a school may be identified as having one or more difficulties which may challenge their learning, e.g. behaviour, ADHD, dyslexia, dyspraxia, visual impairment. It is the school's responsibility to provide these students with Individual Education Plans (IEPs). IEPs are then shared amongst the teaching staff to provide them with additional guidance when teaching these individuals. In any one class you may have a number of students with an IEP. The most efficient way of keeping track of their needs is to write codes in your register next to their name with a key below as an explanation of any recommendations, e.g. sit near the front, make sure glasses are worn, write down homework for them, use 16 point type on worksheets.

What is a Statement of Special Needs?

The Statement is a legal document which the education authority and a child's school must follow. It identifies the help that a child is to be given to meet their special educational needs.

It is in six parts:

1. Important details about the child.
2. Details of all the child's special educational needs.
3. The help which the education authority considers will meet the child's needs.
4. Where the child should go to school.
5. The child's other needs apart from education.
6. How these non-educational needs will be supported.

Students who have been assessed by an educational psychologist as needing additional adult help for their learning difficulty may be 'statemented'. This means that the local authority and school have to provide the child with specific additional help, often in the form of additional hours with an LSA. If the student is statemented they too will have an individual educational plan.

Learning Support Assistants (LSAs)

These men and women are often the unsung heroes in the classroom. LSAs are often allocated to students with IEPs or who are statemented. If you have the honour of having an LSA attached to classes make sure you use them appropriately. LSAs often act as key workers for individuals and as such build good relationships with the student and their family.

● Discuss with your LSA their role in your classroom, i.e. who they are working with.

- Ask them to provide additional information on the student – this maybe helpful when planning.

- If you have a number of students who could benefit from the LSA's help, ask if you can seat certain students next to the target individual so the LSA can help them too.

- Prior to a lesson inform the LSA what you will be teaching.

- If you are wonderfully organised, pass resource materials that you are to use in class to the LSA – they may decide to change it slightly to fit the individual's needs.

- Include the LSA in your lesson – make them feel part of the class – greet them and ask their opinion in front of the students to show that you respect them and therefore so should the class.

- If you have time ask the LSA to feed back on how the lesson went and how their target student got on.

TEACHING REFERENCE

Who is being referred to in educational inclusion?

Educational inclusion is about equal opportunities for all students, whatever their age, ability, ethnicity, gender or background. It tends to focus on particular groups – provision for them and their attainment. The groups may be:

Boys and girls
Minority ethnic or faith groups
Gifted and talented
Children 'looked after'
Special educational needs
Students with English as an Additional Language (EAL)
Students at risk of exclusion
Other children, such as pregnant schoolgirls, young carers, sick children

TEACHING TIPS

'Buddies'

Seat students with a peer or 'buddy' who they can talk to. It is best if this person is more able and has good collaborative skills.

Gifted and Talented (G&T)

According to DCSF guidelines up to 10% of a cohort can be classified as gifted and talented. There is a difference between gifted and talented – but one student may be both. The simple rule is: students who are very good academically are said to be gifted whereas students who excel at sports, performance and creative arts are said to be talented.

Gifted and Talented activities

✔ Let students take the lead
✔ Accelerate their learning – use learning objectives from higher year groups
✔ Set individual objectives and targets
✔ Use peer-coaching
✔ Allocate specific roles in whole class activities
✔ Differentiate questioning/progressive questioning
✔ Group students into ability – giving more challenging work to the gifted and talented

Let students take the lead

This can be done in several ways. Giving part of the lesson over to a student or students is one of the easiest methods. Give the chosen students time to prepare (this might be a homework exercise) and give clear guidance on what they are meant to teach or demonstrate to their peers. Let them be creative – allow them to choose how they do this exercise. The great thing about letting students take over in this way is first, they are using many skills often not used in school, but second, their peers will listen to them more intently than you, the teacher – so give it a go! It saves a bit of planning time too!

Accelerate their learning

Give gifted and talented students different learning objectives. This may sound like extra effort but you can use learning objectives from higher year group SOWs to help. Many schools are now formally introducing accelerated learning with students completing key stages in a shorter period of time.

Set individual objectives and targets

A similar idea to accelerated learning – use higher year objectives to write individual objectives. If this sounds too much, simply provide open-ended tasks that address the objective, allowing the student to develop as far as they can.

Peer-coaching

Students can learn much from one another. A typical example is allowing school team players or county players to carry out warm-ups or umpire games in PE. In classroom environments allow these students to work alongside others so that they can demonstrate their understanding by coaching their peers through the given task.

Allocate specific roles in whole class activities

It is important that the gifted and talented and their peers feel part of the same class and that they are on a similar learning journey. The key is not to make the gifted and talented stand out so as to make them feel embarrassed nor to allow their peers to feel second class citizens next to them. When giving out tasks give gifted and talented students a more challenging slant so that they are doing the work of the rest of the class but are being stretched at the same time. An example could be a class reviewing a poem – the gifted and talented may be asked to compare this poem with others they have read in class.

Differentiate questioning/progressive questioning

In class discussions or question and answer sessions progressively make your questions more challenging. Start by giving basic questions requiring simple recall to your weaker students so that they do not feel left out and get some sense of achievement, then build up the level to questions that require explanations/ predictions, etc.

What do you call . . .?
Where do you find . . .?
Can you describe . . .?
Can you predict . . .?
Can you explain . . .?
Can you make links with . . .?

Group students by ability

Grouping by ability will allow students to work on more challenging work and to bounce ideas off peers of a similar ability.

Personalised Learning (PL)

As defined in the *Gilbert Report of the Teaching and Learning in 2020 Review Group* (2007):

> **Personalised Learning**
> **www.standards.dfes.gov.uk** provides excellent information on the personalised learning agenda.

'Put simply, personalised learning and teaching means taking a highly structured and responsive approach to each child's and young person's learning, in order that all are able to progress, achieve and participate. It means strengthening the link between learning and teaching by engaging pupils – and their parents – as partners in learning.'

So what does PL look like in the classroom?

- Work is varied to meet the different learning styles of individual students.
- Individual data is used to plan and set individual goals for lessons/term/topics, etc.
- LSAs are deployed in class to support students who are not making sufficient progress.
- Intervention is made for students who are struggling – providing additional support/differentiating work/contacting Head of Year/Head of Faculty to see if a whole school strategy is required.
- Parents are informed. Telephone calls/reward letters/concern letters are sent to keep parents in the loop and to allow for the earliest interventions.

Summary

✔ Use Individual Educational Plans (IEPs) to inform your planning.

✔ Work effectively with Learning Support Assistants (LSAs) by sharing lesson plans and ideas.

✔ Challenge your gifted and talented students by allowing them to take the lead, use learning objectives from higher year groups, peer-coach, allocate specific roles in whole class activities, differentiate questioning and group students by ability.

✔ Use data on individuals to plan and set goals. When students are not progressing sufficiently set in place early intervention – additional help, parental involvement.

Further activity

Watch video clips at **www.teachers.tv/video** on SEN, G&T and PL.

Chapter 11

Assessment
for Learning

What I will learn in this chapter?

✔ The difference between 'Assessment *for* Learning' and
  'Assessment *of* Learning'

✔ How to apply assessment for learning in the classroom

✔ Examples of assessment for learning activities

Assessment for Learning aims to raise students' achievement by allowing the students themselves to recognise the aim of their learning and how best they are to achieve this. Importantly, you need to distinguish between 'Assessment *for* Learning' (formative assessment) and 'Assessment *of* Learning' (summative assessment).

'Assessment for Learning is the process of seeking and interpreting evidence for use by learners and their teachers to decide where the learners are in their learning, where they need to go and how best to get there.'

(Assessment Reform Group, 2002: see www.standards.dfes.gov.uk)

Inside the black box

The publication *Inside the Black Box: Raising Standards Through Classroom Assessment* is an influential pamphlet that summarises the main findings of research carried out by Black and Williams. Your school should have copies: if not, ask them to get some in. This is essential reading.

So how does the classroom teacher implement Assessment for Learning (AfL)?

● Share learning objectives and outcomes at the start of a lesson (see Chapter 3).

● Revisit learning objectives and outcomes during the plenary section of a lesson to allow students to see what they have understood so far (see Chapter 7).

● Provide students with guidance so that they recognise the standards to aim for.

● Provide students with self- and peer-assessment opportunities so that they can learn the assessment process rather than just see the final outcome in a grade or comment.

● Mark and assess students' work using language rather than grade or level descriptors to show the students what they have achieved and, importantly, what they must do next to improve.

● Allow students time in the lesson to discuss what they have learnt and how they got to understand the work – metacognition – before allowing them to explain what they need to do next in their learning.

● Use effective questioning techniques (see below).

Sharing learning objectives

As mentioned in Chapter 3 it is no good just reading out the learning objectives at the start of a lesson – you need to explain them in less formal language. Ask students to read out an objective and then explain to them exactly what they will be doing during the lesson in order to achieve the objective. Make sure you make it clear what the objective is and what the task is – students often think simply completing a task is the objective met.

Inform students of what the assessment criteria are – what exactly they need to have done to ensure the objective is achieved.

Make links between what they already know in order to demonstrate to them how this prior knowledge will help them gain the new knowledge and skills hoped for by the end of the lesson.

Learning should be SELF-REGULATED

'Being able to prepare one's own learning, to take the necessary steps to learn, to regulate learning, to provide one's own learning, to provide one's own feedback and performance judgements tend to keep oneself concentrated and motivated.'

(De Cortes, 1995)

Peer and self-assessment

Students need to know what they are required to learn and why. In addition, students need to be actively engaged in assessing their own understanding, what they already know and what they need to know and how they are going to achieve this. This is not as easy as it sounds – students cannot do this without guidance and practice.

Peer assessment

Students love acting as teacher! What they need to do is make sure they are giving constructive feedback and not using the activity to put down their peers. A warning here. Many students are highly embarrassed about their work and have insecurities about their ability. Peer assessment can only be introduced in a 'safe' environment with rules of respect made clear – with consequences for not abiding by the class rules.

Learning should be COOPERATIVE

Since participation in social practices is an essential aspect of situated learning it implies the cooperative nature of productive learning. It accounts for the fact that learners acquire common concepts and skills.

Cobb, Wood and Yackel (1991) considered social interaction essential for mathematics learning,

'with individual knowledge construction occurring throughout processes of interaction, negotiation and cooperation.'

Just as with self-assessment, give the students clear marking criteria to follow.

Self-assessment

Students assessing their own work allows them time to reflect on their learning – similar to how we as teachers should reflect on our own practice at the end of a lesson. However, it does require time and that must be planned for in a lesson.

If students are having problems (and let's face it, reflecting on one's own practice is difficult so think how hard it is for the students) give them time to reflect and problem-solve and provide them with support to cushion their self-esteem.

An excellent way of training pupils in self- and peer assessment is to provide them with examples of anonymous pieces of work (you can make these up or take work from last year's cohort) and let them assess with given criteria. This is a safe way of

Developing constructive feedback

✔ Focus on the learning objectives.

✔ Confirm that the students are on track.

✔ Encourage the correction of errors/improvement of work.

✔ Support students' next steps.

✔ Provide an opportunity for students to think things through.

✔ Avoid comparisons with other students.

✔ Allow students to respond.

introducing assessment for learning and will hopefully help you establish a safe environment for the students to assess their own and their peers' work at a later stage.

Two stars and a wish

When marking or giving feedback teachers must move away from the mark out of ten or a grade/level if they are to implement assessment *for* learning rather than assessment *of* learning. The research rationale is that students focus on marks, grades and levels and rarely read the additional comment. By writing just a comment students are more likely to read it and respond.

A simple method to use in your own marking and when using self- and peer-assessment activities is entitled 'Two stars and a wish'. When giving feedback always start by making two positive comments about their work, i.e. what they have shown they can do, then make a single improvement comment, showing clearly what they need to do.

Using effective questioning techniques

In assessment for learning the term 'high-level questioning' is often thrown around. What this means in the classroom is:

- Find out what students know, understand and can do.

- Analyse students' answers to questions to find out what they know, understand and can do.

- Find out what students' misconceptions are in order to target teaching more effectively.

Examples of good questions

1. How can we be sure that . . .?

2. How do you know . . .?

3. How would you explain what you've described/seen . . .?

4. What does that tell us about . . .?

5. Why is this incorrect . . .?

6. Is this always true/false . . .?

Summary

✔ Assessment for learning is the process of seeking and interpreting evidence for use by learners and their teachers.

✔ Share objectives at the start of a lesson and revisit objectives during the plenary.

✔ Mark and assess work using language rather than grade/level descriptors.

✔ Allow students an opportunity to reflect on their learning.

✔ Encourage students to describe what learning they find difficult and what they find easy – metacognition.

Further activity

Read Black and Williams' (2001) *Inside the Black Box*.

Chapter 12

Homework

What I will learn in this chapter?

✔ How to manage homework marking workload

✔ How to mark effectively

✔ How to set meaningful homework

Homework and the workload it can bring with it can easily destroy the quality of life of teachers new and old who have been unable to get control of this very difficult beast. What you need to remember is that you are contracted for around 37 hours a week – that can be the time some teachers spend marking in one week alone. If you are going to be a successful teacher and have a life outside the classroom you must carefully plan homework so that first, it gets done and second, it is appropriate for your class, but also that it doesn't impinge on your health.

Relate homework to lesson/topic

Make it clear how the homework consolidates or extends work done in class. Go through homework after marking so that students see its relevance. Whilst practising skills is important, homework is most effective when it reinforces main curriculum ideas.

Homework objectives

Not used regularly but perhaps should be! Why not provide students with homework objectives so they can clearly see what it is they are expected to learn from the activity.

How often should I mark?

The first step is to check the school's or faculty's policy on homework and marking. Even if your school has it written that you set homework weekly, for some classes this does not mean you have to mark every piece you set weekly. A common guide is that a secondary school teacher should thoroughly mark one piece of homework each term (six terms in all) and the student's class book once a term – following the Assessment for Learning guidelines (Chapter 11). 'This can't be enough!', you cry – but if done correctly, it is. A primary school teacher will need to view the homework of single class more often – say, once a fortnight or once every three weeks. The key fact is this: there is no point to marking if the feedback is of no use; again, refer to Assessment for Learning. Importantly, if your policy is to set weekly, that does not necessarily mean a different piece of work each week – it could be an assignment that covers the term. However, if you are setting homework over a term or a period of weeks, it is best to give students reminders of the stage they should have reached each week and what the deadline is. Another useful activity to get students to explain what they have done or found out as part of a starter activity to gauge their progress and to encourage others who may have floundered.

Make homework manageable

Homework should challenge students but they also need to be able to complete it successfully. With some classes you will need to differentiate homework to suit abilities.

A final point, but a crucial one. Plan when you are going to mark a class's work in more depth and if you have several classes make sure this is spread out throughout the term. You don't want to leave it to the last week of term to mark six classes' worth of books, neither do you want to spend most of your holiday marking. Referring to Chapter 5 and the use of long-term teaching plans: within these pencil in weeks to mark books – be careful not to mark much (if any) in weeks that are report writing ones. Again, it cannot be emphasised enough the need to plan ahead. If you plan you will manage your time much better – you may not have decided the exact homework you will issue but you know which week you will set it and mark it. It is important to note that the piece you decide to mark in depth needs to be thought out so that it provides you with a good idea of the students' effort and attainment.

Handing in homework

To help you identify who has done homework or not an alternative to reviewing it at the start of the lesson is to ask students to leave the class, one by one, after handing in their homework. Particularly good if a break follows your lesson so you can keep behind those with missing homework and discuss sanctions, etc.

Marking

Provide appropriate feedback

For students to see the importance of homework they must see that their teacher takes it seriously by marking it and returning it as soon as possible.

Feedback must be meaningful and supportive.

Again, your school should have guidelines. Some schools discourage the use of red pen as it is seen as aggressive and ask staff to mark in pencil. Other schools insist you grade the students' effort and attainment. For example, A3 may be used to inform a student that they have applied excellent effort in the piece of work, A, (A-E is the common scale) and the 3 means that they have shown good understanding in the piece but it may have mistakes or lack some further knowledge or skill (scale used here is often 1-5 or 1-10). However, with more and more schools moving to Assessment for Learning this grading is often not necessary and in fact can be a hindrance (see Chapter 11).

Grade/level or comment

When you are marking work either give a grade/level for it or write a comment only. Research shows that whenever a grade/level is given this is where the student focuses their attention – often not bothering to read the comment.

If you do grade/level and comment ensure the student has read the comment by asking them to respond to it.

Peer and self-assessment

As mentioned in Chapter 11, peer and self-assessment are very useful tools that allow students to assess their own and their peers' work, gaining an understanding of what they did well and what they need to do to make improvements in the future. Homework is perfect for this type of assessment. It can be a very effective starter activity. What you need to have in place to ensure its success are clear guidelines on how to mark the work and what students need to be looking for. The traffic light system could be used here as it provides the students and the teacher with an idea of the standard of work. You could provide marking criteria against a level or grade. Remember, it's an ideal time to showcase good pieces of work. However, do encourage students to write comments on their own or peers' books using the 'Two stars and a wish' system. It is crucial that students learn to give back constructive rather than destructive advice as many students will otherwise come to hate this activity and may purposely avoid homework, preferring the sanction instead.

Getting homework in on time

Ever wondered why some teachers can get nearly 100% homework completed by a class week in week out, when other teachers struggle and may get a handful? Follow the tips below and you should fall into the first bracket.

- Set time (preferably at the start) in a lesson to clearly describe the homework and make sure all students have written down details and deadline date in their planner/journal.

- In your register book mark in the date you set the homework and a title so that you can see clearly when it is due and who genuinely was away when it was given out.

- If it is a piece of work to be done over a number of weeks ensure you remind students weekly of what is required and when.

- When taking the register on the day homework is due ask students to simply hold up their work as evidence so that you can see from the start who has done it (however badly) and who has not. As you take the register mark in an 'H' to show homework has been done. Remember, your register can hold more information than simply attendance if used cunningly.

- If some students have failed to do homework, follow the sanctions. Try not to give second chances, e.g. 'Hand it in tomorrow then I won't mark it in as late'. This method will get them into bad habits and not model to them the importance of meeting deadlines – it will also make your marking difficult if books are coming in at different times. Two lates and a sanction is the usual – the sanction may be a detention. My own preference is a phone call home or a letter – parents on your side at home can be all you need to get even repeat offenders' books in on time.

Chase up non-completion of homework

If you fail to pursue non-completion of homework you are reinforcing the view that it was not an important piece of work and gradually more and more of your students will fail to hand in homework.

Making homework appropriate and worthwhile:

1. Make sure the homework is set at a standard that the students are at – if it is too easy or too difficult there is little point setting it.

2. If students have a 30-minute homework, try and keep to that. If students claim they have spent more time than that given you may have set too difficult a task. Encourage students to note in their planners/journals the time spent on their homework.

3. Set differentiated homework or open tasks so that mixed groups are catered for.

Relate homework to everyday life

This helps to make homework relevant and increases the motivation of the students to complete the task.

For example, ask students to interview grandparents who may remember living through a war, etc.

Homework clubs

Many homework clubs come and go – some have been a great hit, some have been a miserable failure. Some schools have clubs available at lunchtime with teachers, teaching assistants or even older students monitoring and helping out. These clubs are often very popular with the more conscientious students who can manage their own time and see the value of getting homework done in school time. However, the clubs that are particularly welcomed are those that are set up specifically for students who have recurrent homework issues: maybe they have no place at home to work, no time (if they are carers) or, in fact, no inclination. These clubs are invitation-only and work when parents are fully involved and can back up this additional school activity. They can be during lunch or after school. The best thing about these clubs is that many students who find work difficult and often do not do their homework are suddenly able to complete this part of school life and, importantly, not get into 'trouble' in class right from the start. It can really help maintain good behaviour as students have done what is expected of them and hopefully feel good about it.

Homework activities

These can be the same as starters and plenary-type activities as shown in Chapters 4 and 6, but what is great about homework is that you have more opportunity to give students the chance to explore a topic further and do some research themselves, rather than just check what they have understood so far. If you do set research work be aware that not all students have access to research tools, e.g. the internet, so you may have to provide the materials. Homework that is finding out about something to be studied in the following lesson is particularly good as it neatly provides you with your next lesson's starter – hence you reduce your planning time and have an opportunity for homework to be marked in class!

Choices homework

Occasionally give students a choice in what homework they could do – particularly at the end of a topic where you wish to revise key concepts, e.g.:

- Write a crossword
- Write a board game
- Write a wordsearch (for low attainers)
- Devise your own testing tool

The great thing about this type of homework is that once again you have a starter activity whereby you simply ask students to swap their homework and to try to complete each other's tasks – they really enjoy this.

Summary

✔ Plan when you are going to mark.

✔ Don't mark every piece of homework formally – use peer and self-assessment in class to review this work.

✔ Mark formally regularly – say once a term per subject – in order to give students specific advice. Use the 'Two stars and a wish' method to mark.

✔ Either write a comment or give a grade/level – research shows that students focus on grades/levels and pay little attention to the comment unless it is written without an accompanying grade.

✔ Chase up missing homework – don't let this go unnoticed or without sanction. Get parents involved.

✔ Support homework clubs and encourage students to attend.

Further activity

When writing homework activities attempt to write objectives alongside to guide the students – similar to lesson objectives. This will help you and the students assess their success with this type of activity.

Bibliography

Bandura, A. (1977) *Social Learning Theory*, Prentice Hall, Englewood Cliffs.

Beaman, R. and Wheldall, K. (2000) 'Teachers' Use of Approval and Disapproval in the Classroom', *Educational Psychology*, 20 (4), 431–446.

Black, P. and Williams, D. (2001) *Inside the Black Box*, BERA Short Final Draft, King's College London.

Bloom, B. S. (1956) *Taxonomy of Educational Objectives*, Handbook I: The Cognitive Domain, David McKay Co Inc., New York.

Cobb, P., Wood, T. and Yackel, E. (1991) 'Change in Teaching Mathematics', *American Educational Research Journal* (28) 587–616.

Croll, P. and Moses, D. (2000) *Special Needs in the Primary Classroom: One in Five*, Cassell Academic, London.

De Cortes, E. (1995) 'Fostering Educational Growth', *Educational Psychologist* (30) 37–46.

Fisher, P. (2001) *Thinking through History*, Chris Kington Publishing, Cambridge.

Gagne, R. (1985) *The Conditions of Learning and Theory of Instruction, 4th edition*, Holt, Rinehart and Winston, New York.

Gilbert, C. (2006) *Vision 2020: Report of the Teaching and Learning in 2020 Review Group* (DFES).

Ginott, H. (1972) *Teacher and Child*, Macmillan and Co Ltd, London.

Hargreaves, D. (1967) *Social Relations in a Secondary School*, Routledge & Kegan Paul Ltd, London.

Morrow, L. and Weinstein, C. (1982) 'Relationships between Literature Programs, Library Corner Designs and Children's Use of Literature', *Educational Journal of Research* (75) 339–344.

Mujis, D. and Reynolds, D. (2001) *Effective Teaching: Evidence and Practice*. Paul Chapman Educational Publishing, London.

Olson, D. and Torrance, N. (1998) *The Handbook of Education and Human Development*, Blackwell, Oxford.

Rogers, B. (2006) *Cracking the Hard* Class, *2nd edition*, Paul Chapman Educational Publishing, London.

Rosenshine, B. (1979) 'Content, Time, and Direct Instruction' in *Research on Teaching: Concepts, Findings and Implications*, (eds) P. Peterson and H. Walburg, McCutchan, Berkeley.

Vygotsky, L. S. (1978) *Mind in Society*, Harvard University Press, Cambridge, MA.

Index